"I laughed so hard and uncontrolla
public transport is not a good idea. n

Kate Huchinson, editor, Penthouse magazine

"I had to look away I was laughing so hard. Hands down the funniest emails I have ever read."

Catherine DiBenedetto, editor, WIRED Magazine

"The Dennis the Menace of the internet, Thorne's intricately woven web of internet tomfoolery is guaranteed to leave you red-faced from laughter."

Matt Bachl, ninemsn TV news producer

"The world's leading internet troublemaker. Whenever I see David Thorne's name, I know it's going to be a long day at the office."

Andrew Ramadge, editor, news.com.au

"In the dominion of social networking and electronic communication, David Thorne has become the king of biting sarcasm."

Thane Burnett, editor, Sun Media

"The most ridiculous, brilliant, stupid and clever nonsense I have ever come across. The articles had me rolling with laughter, crying and incapable of speaking - my co-workers thought I had gone insane."

Clare Butchard, associate producer, Hat Trick Productions UK

"Gut wrenching, laugh out loud, gasping for air funny. Absolutely brilliant."

Caroline Shaheed, editor, Cheek Magazine

"Thorne's ability to manipulate the websphere with his touch of serious sarcasm has surely earned him the moniker 'Lord of the Viral Email'. I've seen grown men reduced to hysterical tears of laughter after reading through just one of his efforts."

Matty Soccio, editor, Marketing magazine

"I am getting your website banned as we speak"

Lucius Thaller, Courier, Kings Transport

"Adelaide is full of selfish, petty, judgmental, cocooned, insular, naive people totally devoid of social consciousness or culture and David Thorne is their spokesperson."

Roz Knorr, woman golfer, Seocontents.net

the internet is a playground

david thorne

FONTAINE
PRESS

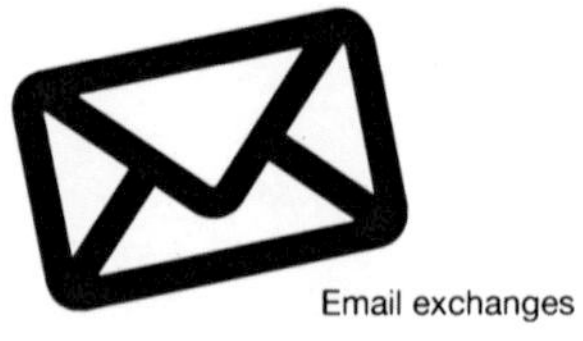

Published by Fontaine Press
P.O. Box 948, Fremantle
Western Australia 6959
www.fontainepress.com

FOREWORD

by Andrew Ramadge, Technology Editor, news.com.au

It's a pretty good time to be a tech journo. Not since the invention of the printing press or the telephone has technology changed the ways that we communicate with and relate to each other so drastically. The pace of change has been so fast that laws and culture have yet to catch up. We are still struggling to understand the impact that the internet – and the world wide web, email and file-sharing along with it – has had on our world.

Since becoming news.com.au's first reporter dedicated to covering technology, I have written about the roll-out of Google Street View, a virtual recreation of every street corner that just two decades ago would have been imagined science fiction; the privacy implications of sharing our lives on social networking sites like Facebook; and the Rudd Government's plan to build a $43 billion dollar fibre optic broadband network, the largest infrastructure project in Australia's history.

However none of these incredibly important and interesting things excited readers quite as much as a wonky picture of an arachnid. My first interview with David Thorne, after emails documenting his attempt to pay a bill with a drawing of a seven-legged spider went around the world, was one of the most popular technology stories ever to run on news.com.au. In it, the prankster talked of amusing and annoying people and using the internet as a "playground".

To computer nerds, Thorne is the latest star in the sport of "trolling" – a favourite pastime of tech-savvy troublemakers who delight in eliciting the anger of those who believe the internet to be "serious business". But for perhaps the first time, everyone else wanted to follow the story as well. Thorne's exploits aren't limited to a niche audience of geeks – they say something about everyday life that we can all relate to.

Thorne uses technology to undermine our social norms, from party etiquette to having pets in apartments and shopping at IKEA, with his pranks via email and social networking sites like Facebook and MySpace. Just as we are getting used to the idea that emails may be binding, that legal notices may be delivered by direct message, Thorne is here to remind us, sometimes rudely, that not everything you read on the internet is true.

Pray you don't see his name pop up in your Inbox.

Andrew Ramadge

For Holly & Seb

INTRODUCTION

27bslash6.com started simply to annoy people, it averaged around fifty hits a week until boredatwork.com posted the article 'If I had a monkey' in late 2008 and the hits went up to around five thousand a week. When the article I wrote featuring correspondence between myself and Jane in regards to paying an account with a drawing of a spider was posted on Digg and Reddit, my servers crashed from being hit by many hundreds of thousands of visitors and the website has enjoyed high numbers since. The format of the spider email was easy to copy and paste so effectively went viral overnight. Following this, an associate added to the media interest by selling the spider on eBay. Getting caught up in the fun, Patrick Munoz placed a bid for US$10,000 and unfortunately for him, won. This, and the following refusal of Patrick to pay, was picked up and reported on commercial news sites such as nine.msn and news.com, which added to and continued the popularity of the original story. I believe eBay gave him a red strike or small electric shock or whatever it is they do in these instances but that is preferable to paying fifteen grand for something anybody can copy and paste if they are inclined. The story on the sale did quote me as saying "The internet is a playground and I would not have it any other way" which made me sound cool so that was nice.

The content in this collection purposely has no point and I have found that this pointlessness seems to be its main appeal. As much of the content comes from attempting to distract myself, the stories that have distracted me the most are my favourites. Playing with a very heated Dick provided me many hours of entertainment but I have enjoyed all of them or they would not exist. If I was really being honest, I would have to say the flight commander article is my favourite because I wish I was an astronaut but as that would make me sound like a geek, I won't.

Thanks go to my offspring Seb for his part in the inanity, he is very annoying at times but unless I am offered a very good price, will keep him. Holly, my favourite person on the whole planet despite her being American. Ross for being funny and a good friend. Gina, Mark, Simon, Leith & Craig for good beer and company and last and most certainly least, Bill for never cracking a smile no matter what I write.

A big thankyou also goes to the people who link to, tweet, re-post and frequent the 27bslash6 website. Without them, the hit counters would only be in the double digits.

Hello! My name is Matthew and I have moved into Apartment 3. I m having a house warming party next week on the 14th, if the noise gets to loud that night let me know. Nice to meet you anyhow let me know if you ever need anything.
Cheers Matthew

mobile 04 [illegible]
email matthews [illegible] .au

DEAR NEIGHBOUR YOU ARE NOT INVITED TO MY PARTY

A few weeks ago, a guy moved into the apartment across from me. I know little about him apart from the fact that he owns cane furniture as I saw the delivery guys carry it up. I bumped into him on the stairs once and he said hello but I cannot be friends with someone that owns cane furniture so I pretended I had a turtle to feed or something.

Last week when I checked my mailbox, I found that my new neighbour had left me a note stating that he was having a party and to let him know if the noise was too loud. The problem I have with the note is not that he was having a party and didn't invite me, it was that he selected a vibrant background of balloons, effectively stating that his party was going to be vibrant and possibly have balloons and that I couldn't come. If I was writing a note to my neighbours saying that I was going to have a party but none of them could come, I would not add photos of ecstasy tablets, beer and gratuitous shots of Lucius going down on men to show them what they are missing out on, I would make it clean and simple, possibly even sombre, so they didn't think 'you prick'.

From: David Thorne
Date: Monday 8 Dec 2008 11.04am
To: Matthew Smythe
Subject: R.S.V.P.

Dear Matthew,

Thankyou for the party invite. At first glance I thought it may be a child's party what with it being vibrant and having balloons but I realise you probably did your best with what little tools were available. I wouldn't miss it for the world. What time would you like me there?

Regards, David.

From: Matthew Smythe
Date: Monday 8 Dec 2008 3.48pm
To: David Thorne
Subject: Re: R.S.V.P.

Hi David
Sorry the note was just to let you know that we might be a bit loud that night. The house warming is really just for friends and family but you can drop past for a beer if you like.
Cheers Matthew

From: David Thorne
Date: Monday 8 Dec 2008 5.41pm
To: Matthew Smythe
Subject: Re: Re: R.S.V.P.

Thanks Matthew,

Including me in your list of friends and family means a lot. You and I don't tend to have long discussions when we meet in the hallway and I plan to put a stop to that. Next time we bump into each other I intend to have a very long conversation with you and I am sure you are looking forward to that as much as I am. I have told my friend Ross that you are having a party and he is as excited as I am. Do you want us to bring anything or will everything be provided?

Regards, David.

From: Matthew Smythe
Date: Tuesday 9 Dec 2008 10.01am
To: David Thorne
Subject: Re: Re: Re: R.S.V.P.

Hi David
As I said, my housewarming is just for friends and family. There is not a lot of room so cant really have to many people come. Sorry about that mate.
Cheers Matthew

From: David Thorne
Date: Tuesday 9 Dec 2008 2.36pm
To: Matthew Smythe
Subject: Re: Re: Re: Re: R.S.V.P.

Dear Matthew,

I can appreciate that, our apartments are not very large are they? I myself like to go for a jog every night to keep fit but fear leaving the house so I have to jog on the spot taking very small steps with my arms straight down. I understand the problems of space restrictions all too well. If you would like to store some of your furniture at my place during the party you are quite welcome to - if we move your cane furniture into my spare room for the night and scatter cushions on the ground, that would provide a lot more seating and create a cozy atmosphere at the same time. I have a mirror ball that you can borrow. I have told Ross not to invite anyone else due to the space constraints so it will just be us two and my other friend Simon. When I told Simon that Ross and I were going to a party he became quite angry that I had not invited him as well so I really didn't have any choice as he can become quite violent. Sometimes I am afraid to even be in the same room as him. So just myself, Ross and Simon. Simon's girlfriend has a work function on that night but might come along after that if she can get a lift with friends.

Regards, David.

From: Matthew Smythe
Date: Tuesday 9 Dec 2008 4.19pm
To: David Thorne
Subject: Re: Re: Re: Re: Re: R.S.V.P.

Wtf? Nobody can come to the houswarming party it is just for friends and family. I dont even know these people. How do you know I have cane furniture? Are you the guy in apartment 1?

From: David Thorne
Date: Tuesday 9 Dec 2008 6.12pm
To: Matthew Smythe
Subject: Re: Re: Re: Re: Re: Re: R.S.V.P.

Hi Matthew,

I understand it is an exclusive party and I appreciate you trusting my judgement on who to bring. I just assumed you have cane furniture, doesn't everybody? Cane is possibly one of the most renewable natural resources we have after plastic, it is not only strong but lightweight and attractive. Every item in my apartment is made of cane, including my television. It looks like the one from Gilligan's Island but is in colour of course. Do you remember that episode where a robot came to the island? That was the best one in my opinion. I always preferred Mary Anne to Ginger, same with Flintstones - I found Betty much more attractive than Wilma but then I am not really keen on redheads at all. They have freckles all over their body did you know? It's the ones on their back and shoulders that creep me out the most.

Anyway, Ross rang me today all excited about the party and asked me what the theme is, I told him that I don't think there is a theme and we discussed it and feel that it should be an eighties themed party. I have a white suit and projector and am coming as Nik Kershaw. I have made a looping tape of 'wouldn't it be good' to play as I am sure you will agree that this song rocks and has stood the test of time well. I am in the process of redesigning your invites appropriately and will get a few hundred of them printed off later today. I will have to ask you for the money for this as print cartridges for my Epson are pretty expensive. They stopped making this model a month after I bought it and I have to get the cartridges sent from China. Around $120 should cover it. You can just pop the money in my letter box if I don't see you before tonight.

Regards, David.

From: Matthew Smythe
Date: Wednesday 10 Dec 2008 11.06pm
To: David Thorne
Subject: Re: Re: Re: Re: Re: Re: Re: R.S.V.P.

What the fuck are yout alking about? There is no theme for the party it is just a few friends and family. noone else can come IT IS ONLY FOR MY FRIENDS AND FAMILY do you understand? Do not print anything out because I am not paying for something I dont need and didnt ask you to do! look I am sorry but i am heaps busy and that night is not convenient. Are you in Apatrment1?

From: David Thorne
Date: Thursday 11 Dec 2008 9.15am
To: Matthew Smythe
Subject: Re: Re: Re: Re: Re: Re: Re: Re: R.S.V.P.

Hello Matthew,

I agree that it is not very convenient and must admit that when I first received your invitation I was perplexed that it was on a Sunday night but who am I to judge? No, I am in apartment 3B. Our bedroom walls are touching so when we are sleeping our heads are only a few feet apart. If I put my ear to the wall I can hear you. I also agree with you that having a particular theme for your party may not be the best choice, it makes more sense to leave it open as a generic fancy dress party, that way everyone can come dressed in whatever they want. Once, I went to a party in a bear outfit which worked out well as it was freezing and I was the only one warm. As it won't be cold the night of your party, I have decided to come as a ninja. I think it would be really good if you dressed as a ninja as well and we could perform a martial arts display for the other guests. I have real swords and will bring them. If you need help with your costume let me know, I have made mine by wrapping a black t-shirt around my face with a hooded jacket and cut finger holes in black socks for the gloves. I do not have any black pants so will spray paint my legs on the night.

It is a little hard to breathe in the costume so I will need you to keep the window open during the party to provide good air circulation. Actually, I just had a thought, how awesome would it be if I arrived 'through' the window like a real ninja. We should definitely do that. I just measured the distance between our balconies and I should be able to jump it. I once leaped across a creek that was over five metres wide and almost made it.

Also, you mentioned in your invitation that if there was anything I needed, to let you know. My car is going in for a service next week and I was wondering, seeing as we are good friends now, if it would be ok to borrow yours on that day? I hate catching the bus as they are full of poor people who don't own cars.

Regards, David.

From: Matthew Smythe
Date: Thursday 11 Dec 2008 3.02pm
To: David Thorne
Subject: Re: Re: Re: Re: Re: Re: Re: Re: Re: R.S.V.P.

WTF? No you cant borrow my car and there is no fucking 3B. I reckon you are that guy from Apartment 1. You are not coming to my house warming and you are not bringing any of your friends. What the fuck is wrong with you??? The only people invited are friends and family I told you that. It is just drinks there is no fucking fancy dress and only people i know are coming! I dont want to be rude but jesus fucking christ man.

From: David Thorne
Date: Sunday 14 Dec 2008 2.04am
To: Matthew Smythe
Subject: Party

Hello Matthew,

I have been away since Thursday so have not been able to check my email from home. Flying back late today in time for the party and just wanted to say that we are really looking forward to it. Will probably get there around eleven or twelve, just when it starts to liven up. Simon's girlfriend Cathy's work function was cancelled so she can make it afterall which is good news. She will probably have a few friends with her so they will take the minivan. Also, I have arranged a Piñata.

Regards, David.

Simon Edhouse from the Virtusoft corporation has created this model to illustrate how a "home computer" could look like in the year 2010. Although the needed technology will not be economically feasible for the average home and Mr Edhouse admits that the computer will require not yet invented technology to actually work, scientific progress is expected to solve these problems. With teletype interface and the Fortran language, Mr Edhouse envisions the computer will be easy to use.

PLEASE DESIGN A LOGO FOR ME
WITH PIE CHARTS FOR FREE

I quite like Simon, he is like the school teacher that would pull you aside after class and list, for an hour, every bad aspect of your personality and why you will never get anywhere while you nod and pretend to listen while thinking about how tight Sally Watts jeans were that day and wishing you were at home playing Choplifter on the family's new Amstrad.

I worked with Simon for a while at a branding agency. He was employed to bring in new clients yet somehow managed to be there for several months without bringing in a single one before leaving to pursue his own projects. The lack of new clients may possibly be attributed to his being too busy writing angry emails to other de Masi jones employees such as "When I worked at Olgilvy in Hong Kong, everyone called me Mr Edhouse and said that I was doing a great job. Not once did the secretary there call me a wanker or have her grotty old g-strings poking out the top of her fat arse everyday making me feel ill." which I found much more entertaining than having to do the work new clients would have entailed.

From: Simon Edhouse
Date: Monday 16 November 2009 2.19pm
To: David Thorne
Subject: Logo Design

Hello David,
I would like to catch up as I am working on a really exciting project at the moment and need a logo designed. Basically something representing peer to peer networking. I have to have something to show prospective clients this week so would you be able to pull something together in the next few days? I will also need a couple of pie charts done for a 1 page website. If deal goes ahead there will be some good money in it for you.
Simon

From: David Thorne
Date: Monday 16 November 2009 3.52pm
To: Simon Edhouse
Subject: Re: Logo Design

Dear Simon,

Disregarding the fact that you have still not paid me for work I completed earlier this year despite several assertions that you would do so, I would be delighted to spend my free time creating logos and pie charts for you based on further vague promises of future possible payment. Please find attached pie chart as requested and let me know of any changes required.

Regards, David.

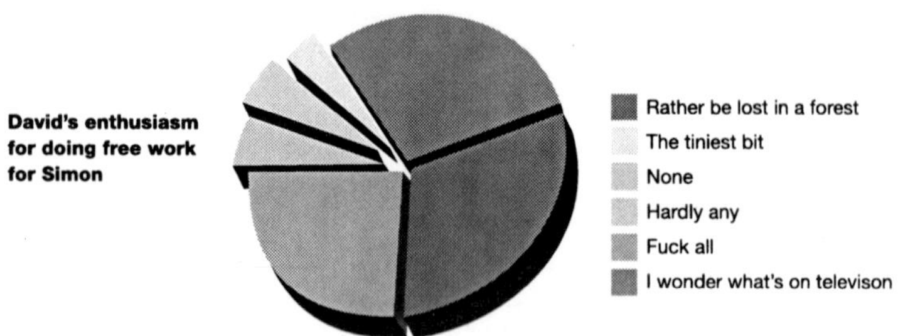

From: Simon Edhouse
Date: Monday 16 November 2009 4.11pm
To: David Thorne
Subject: Re: Re: Logo Design

Is that supposed to be a fucking joke? I told you the previous projects did not go ahead. I invested a lot more time and energy in those projects than you did. If you put as much energy into the projects as you do being a dickhead you would be a lot more successful.

From: David Thorne
Date: Monday 16 November 2009 5.27pm
To: Simon Edhouse
Subject: Re: Re: Re: Logo Design

Dear Simon,

You are correct and I apologise. Your last project was actually both commercially viable and original. Unfortunately the part that was commercially viable was not original, and the part that was original was not commercially viable.

I would no doubt find your ideas more 'cutting edge' and original if I had traveled forward in time from the 1950's but as it stands, your ideas for technology based projects that have already been put into application by other people several years before you thought of them fail to generate the enthusiasm they possibly deserve. Having said that though, if I had traveled forward in time, my time machine would probably put your peer to peer networking technology to shame as not only would it have commercial viability, but also an awesome logo and accompanying pie charts.

Regardless, I have, as requested, attached a logo that represents not only the peer to peer networking project you are currently working on, but working with you in general.

Regards, David.

From: Simon Edhouse
Date: Tuesday 17 November 2009 11.07am
To: David Thorne
Subject: Re: Re: Re: Re: Logo Design

You just crossed the line. You have no idea about the potential this project has. The technology allows users to network peer to peer, add contacts, share information and is potentially worth many millions of dollars and your short sightedness just cost you any chance of being involved.

From: David Thorne
Date: Tuesday 17 November 2009 1.36pm
To: Simon Edhouse
Subject: Re: Re: Re: Re: Re: Logo Design

Dear Simon,

So you have invented Twitter. Congratulations. This is where that time machine would definitely have come in quite handy.

When I was about twelve, I read that time slows down when approaching the speed of light so I constructed a time machine by securing my father's portable generator to the back of my mini-bike with rope and attaching the drive belt to the back wheel. Unfortunately, instead of traveling through time and finding myself in the future, I traveled about fifty metres along the footpath at 200mph before finding myself in a bush. When asked by the nurse filling out the hospital accident report "Cause of accident?" I stated 'time travel attempt' but she wrote down 'stupidity'.

If I did have a working time machine, the first thing I would do is go back four days and tell myself to read the warning on the hair removal cream packaging where it recommends not using on sensitive areas. I would then travel several months back to warn myself against agreeing to do copious amounts of design work for an old man wielding the business plan equivalent of a retarded child poking itself in the eye with a spoon, before finally traveling back to 1982 and explaining to myself the long term photographic repercussions of going to the hairdresser and asking for a haircut exactly like Simon LeBon's the day before a large family gathering.

Regards, David.

From: Simon Edhouse
Date: Tuesday 17 November 2009 3.29pm
To: David Thorne
Subject: Re: Re: Re: Re: Re: Re: Logo Design

You really are a fucking idiot and have no idea what you are talking about. The project I am working on will be more successful than twitter within a year. When I sell the project for 40 million dollars I will ignore any emails from you begging to be a part of it and will send you a postcard from my yaght. Ciao.

From: David Thorne
Date: Tuesday 17 November 2009 3.58pm
To: Simon Edhouse
Subject: Re: Re: Re: Re: Re: Re: Re: Logo Design

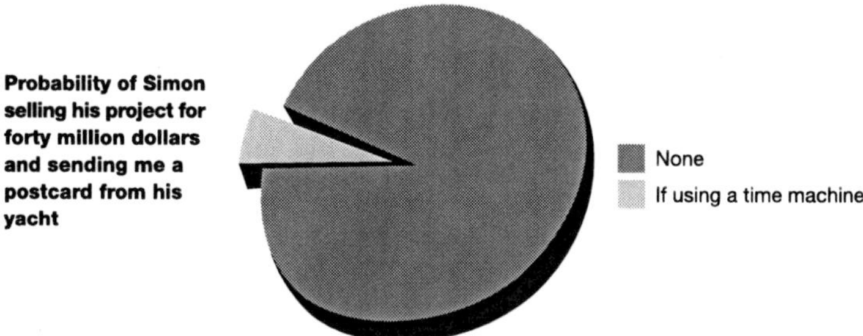

From: Simon Edhouse
Date: Tuesday 17 November 2009 4.10pm
To: David Thorne
Subject: Re: Re: Re: Re: Re: Re: Re: Re: Logo Design

Anyone else would be able to see the opportunity I am presenting but not you. You have to be a fucking smart arse about it. All I was asking for was a logo and a few pie charts which would have taken you a few fucking hours.

From: David Thorne
Date: Tuesday 17 November 2009 4.25pm
To: Simon Edhouse
Subject: Re: Re: Re: Re: Re: Re: Re: Re: Re: Logo Design

Dear Simon

Actually, you were asking me to design a logotype which would have taken me a few hours and fifteen years experience. For free. With pie charts. Usually when people don't ask me to design them a logo, pie charts or website, I, in return, do not ask them to paint my apartment, drive me to the airport, represent me in court or whatever it is they do for a living. Unfortunately though, as your business model consists entirely of "Facebook is cool, I am going to make a website just like that", this non exchange of free services has no foundation as you offer nothing of which I wont ask for.

Regards, David.

From: Simon Edhouse
Date: Tuesday 17 November 2009 4.43pm
To: David Thorne
Subject: Re: Re: Re: Re: Re: Re: Re: Re: Re: Re: Logo Design

What the fuck is your point? Are you going to do the logo and charts for me or not?

From: David Thorne
Date: Tuesday 17 November 2009 5.02pm
To: Simon Edhouse
Subject: Re: Re: Re: Re: Re: Re: Re: Re: Re: Re: Re: Logo Design

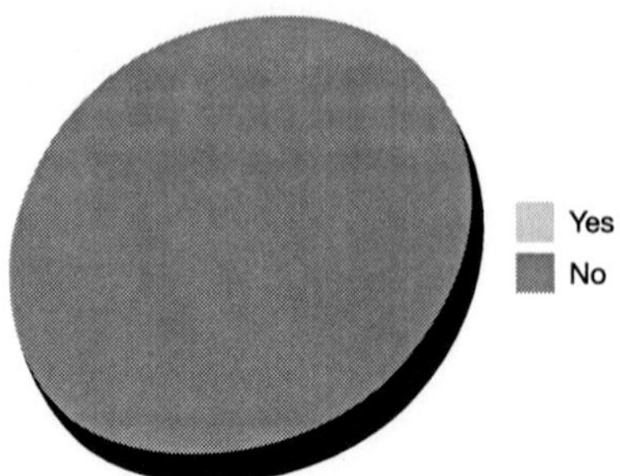

From: Simon Edhouse
Date: Tuesday 17 November 2009 5.13pm
To: David Thorne
Subject: Re: Re: Re: Re: Re: Re: Re: Re: Re: Re: Re: Re: Logo Design
Do not ever email me again.

From: David Thorne
Date: Tuesday 17 November 2009 5.19pm
To: Simon Edhouse
Subject: Re: Re: Re: Re: Re: Re: Re: Re: Re: Re: Re: Re: Re: Logo Design

Ok. Good luck with your project. If you need anything let me know.
Regards, David.

From: Simon Edhouse
Date: Tuesday 17 November 2009 5.27pm
To: David Thorne
Subject: Re: Re: Re: Re: Re: Re: Re: Re: Re: Re: Re: Re: Re: Re: Logo Design

Get fucked.

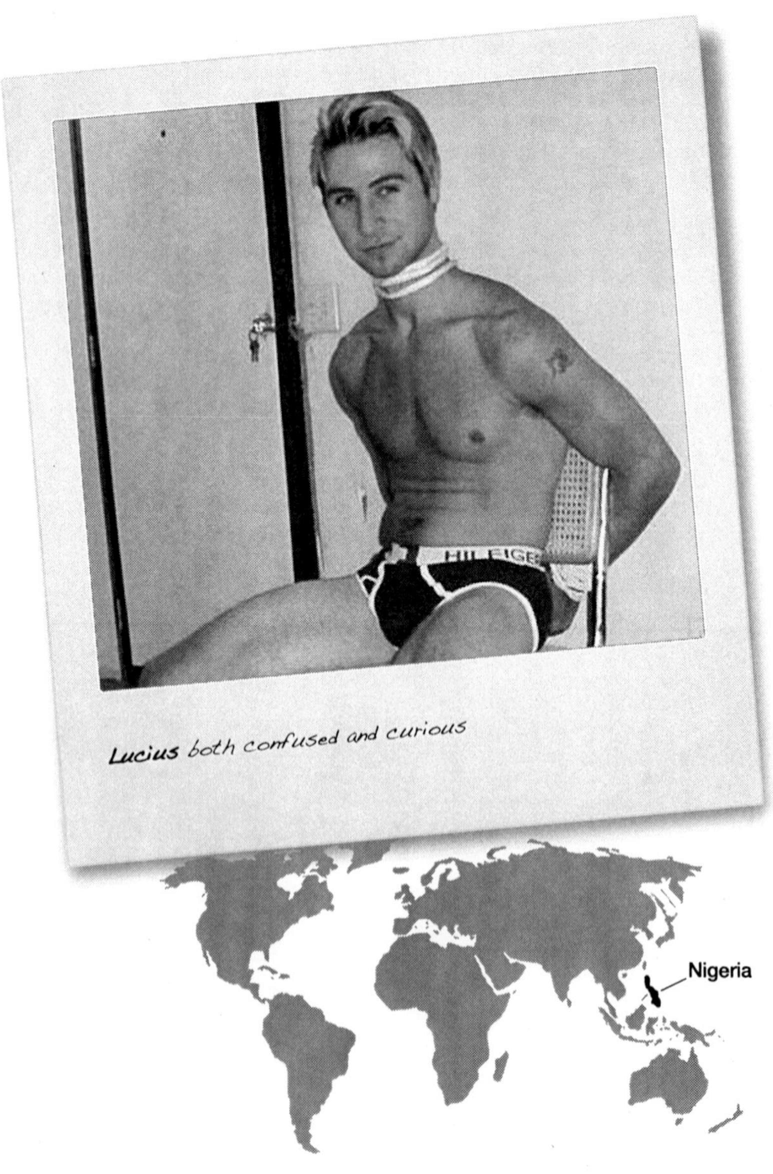

Lucius both confused and curious

LUCIUS CAUGHT IN NIGERIAN EMAIL SEX SCAM

Local captain of most teams, including the lucius fan club, is safe after his 'safari to riches' became a living nightmare. Replying to the email was his first mistake. A mistake that would cost Lucius more than the amount he gave to Mr Bandabaloobi.

"Mr Bandabaloobi said he was from the Nigerian Bank" said Lucius "We first met when he wrote me an email explaining he needed me to transfer three million dollars out of the country because a rich old guy had died and the government was going to keep the money unless I could help and for this I would receive a percentage."

"I gave them my account details and bought a plane ticket to Nigeria to meet Mr Bandabaloobi and sign the transfer papers."

"Once I arrived I was beaten and taken to a small hotel room on the outskirts of town. I was stripped and kissed by dark and very hairy men. One of the men, named Carl, was very gentle and told me he loved me but the others were rough. So very rough. I struggled and told them I was a friend of Mr Bandabaloobi but they tied me up and took turns kissing my beautiful body, touching me and making me do things I had sometimes thought about and imagined, but had never expected to really happen because I am straight. The fact that one of the men looked like a black version of my dad kind of freaked me out and Carl turned out to be huge but like I said, he was very gentle and we just took things really slow. He's cool, we have swapped emails since. Nothing gay though, cause he knows I am straight."

"Having survived the ordeal and returned home, my only regret is that I missed my meeting with Mr Bandabaloobi and didnt get to see any African animals like giraffes and lions and those little things that peek up really quick and look around and then pop back down really quick. They are really cool. They are like those little dogs that live on the prairie. Can't remember what those ones are called either but they look a little bit like otters. They dont live in water like otters though, they live on the prairies. No, I dont know what a prairie is."

Light fitment broken.

D34

OWNER:	Z Vulic	INSPECTION DATE:	30.9.09
TENANT:	THORNE / DAVID	INSPECTION BY:	Peter
PROPERTY ADDRESS:	[redacted]		

	G	A	P	COMMENTS/SUGGESTIONS
ENTRY HALL				
PASSAGES				
LOUNGE ROOM				woodwork requires cleaning
DINING ROOM				including front door
KITCHEN		✓		tiles grubby.
FAMILY ROOM				Stove burners req. cleaning
BEDROOM 1		✓		
BEDROOM 2		✓		
BEDROOM 3		✓		
BEDROOM 4				
STUDY				
BATHROOM				shower base grubby,
ENSUITE		✓		extractor fan filthy.
TOILET 1				
TOILET 2				
LAUNDRY				
GARAGE/CARPORT				
SHED/W.SHOP				
PATIO				
POOL				
FRONT GARDEN				
REAR GARDEN				Side fence has been replaced
WATER METER				

GENERAL COMMENTS

Property is not being maintained to a satisfactory condition.
walls, paintwork, tiles all require cleaning.
Apartment smells of smoke; This is a no smoking tenancy agreement

G - GOOD A - AVERAGE P - POOR

Property to be Re-Inspected in two weeks time.

DEAR TENANT
YOU ARE GRUBBY AND SMELL OF SMOKE

Peter's profile on his company's website declares that Peter, an assistant rental manager, enjoys cricket and coin collecting. And once swam with sharks. These conflicting pastimes puzzled me until I got to where he listed Flowers in the Attic by Virginia Andrews as his favourite novel and I realised he was simply insane.

I am not a great fan of rental property inspections but they are preferrable to rental property inspections without warning. Especially if you are not home at the time. And you haven't cleaned since a four day binge of beer, cigarettes and internet. And you have an adult movie cover left on top of the television in the bedroom. Next to drugs.

One of the worst adult movies I have ever seen was called Debbie Does Dallas which featured a lot of scenes with people wearing clothes and talking about things and, because the movie was shot in the seventies, looked like they were wearing pants made out of hair when they finally did get naked.The worst adult movie I have ever seen was titled Marge & Me Xmas 94 which I found inside a second hand Betamax video recorder I bought for thirty five dollars. While it contained a lot of nudity, most of it hairless, and very little dialogue apart from Marge complaining continuously about a cramp and at one point the gas bill, they were both extremely overweight and well into their sixties so I could only handle an hour or so before ejecting in disgust.

From: David Thorne
Date: Wednesday 30 September 2009 6.04pm
To: Peter Williams
Subject: Inspection Report

Dear Peter,

Thankyou for the surprise inspection and invitation to participate in the next. I appreciate you underlining the text at the bottom of the page which I would otherwise have surely mistaken for part of the natural pattern in the paper. I was going to clean the apartment but had so many things on my 'to do' list that I decided to treat them all equally and draw pictures of sharks instead. I have attached one for your honest appraisal.

Regards, David.

From: Peter Williams
Date: Thursday 01 October 2009 9.41am
To: David Thorne
Subject: Re: Inspection Report

David

I recommed you take this matter more seriously. You were sent notice of the inspection as part of our normal procedure. In addition to the cleaning, the light fitting in the lounge room is broken and the apartment smells of smoke.

Peter

From: David Thorne
Date: Thursday 01 October 2009 10.26am
To: Peter Williams
Subject: Re: Re: Inspection Report

Dear Peter,

The light fitting was the victim of a toy lightsabre being swung in a space too small to do the same with a cat. I dodged a leaping double handed overhead attack and the fitting, being fitted, didn't. I will grab a matching replacement $12 fitting from IKEA the next time I require a tiny ironing board or glass tea light.

The smell you mistook for cigarette smoke was probably just from the fog machine. Each Tuesday I hold a disco in my bedroom with strobe lighting and special guest. As my wardrobe door has a large mirror on it, it looks like someone is dancing with you. I once dressed as a lady and it was almost exactly what I imagine dancing with a real lady would be like. Unfortunately, I kept worrying about falling, hitting my head and being found dressed that way so she left after only a few dances and a brief kiss. You should come one night, it will be a dance spectacular. I imagine you are probably a good dancer because you are small and the smallest member of the Rocksteady Crew was definitely the best one.

Regards, David.

From: Peter Williams
Date: Thursday 01 October 2009 1.16pm
To: David Thorne
Subject: Re: Re: Re: Inspection Report

David

I do not appreciate being called small and being sent stupid drawings of me being eaten by a shark. The apartment is to be cleaned and reinspected in two weeks time. You cant have a fog machine or anything like that at the apartment in case the smoke damages the walls.

Peter

From: David Thorne
Date: Thursday 01 October 2009 4.02pm
To: Peter Williams
Subject: Re: Re: Re: Re: Inspection Report

Dear Peter,

I apologise for mentioning your smallness. It must be a subject most people you know avoid. Was it the Rocksteady Crew comment or the fact that the shark was actually very small in the picture, making you, in comparison, the size of a very small fish? I have attached a revised version which you can print out, pin to your cubicle wall, look at whenever you are feeling down and think "That Volkswagen looks way too small for me to get into, I must be huge."

Regards, David.

From: Peter Williams
Date: Thursday 01 October 2009 5.12pm
To: David Thorne
Subject: Re: Re: Re: Re: Re: Inspection Report

David

Do not send me anymore drawings. I am not joking. I am keeping a record of everything you send just so you know. If the apartment is not clean when we reinspect in two weeks time, we will consider terminating the lease as we have also had ongoing noise complaints regarding the premises.

Peter

From: David Thorne
Date: Thursday 01 October 2009 6.27pm
To: Peter Williams
Subject: Re: Re: Re: Re: Re: Re: Inspection Report

Dear Peter,

Yes, I find loud music helps me relax while I clean as the music distracts me so much that I stop cleaning. Which is relaxing. I will probably get onto it this week though as I do not wish to be evicted. I have developed a severe case of agoraphobia and residing in an apartment where I can reach all four walls while standing in the one spot brings me a feeling of security and the daily culling of plague proportion cockroaches gives me something to do in my spare time. I class the eighteen cans of surface spray I use per week as sporting equipment.

I purchased one of those electronic things that plugs into the wall which is meant to scare cockroaches by sending a pulse through the apartment wiring but while it has reduced the numbers, it seems others have evolved to feed off the electrical signal, increasing their size. I am using one as a coffee table in the lounge and two smaller ones as side tables in the bedroom. They would probably be susceptible to carbon monoxide poisoning though so I will try running a hose pipe from my car exhaust to the apartment, closing the windows and leaving the vehicle running overnight. It is apparently an odourless gas so should not prove an issue for my son's cub group sleepover. Also, I read somewhere once that cockroaches can survive a nuclear attack so I have been collecting the dead ones and intend to glue several thousand to the walls thereby ensuring my survival should Cyberdyne Systems become self aware between now and when the lease runs out.

Regards, David.

From: Peter Williams
Date: Friday 02 October 2009 10.18am
To: David Thorne
Subject: Re: Re: Re: Re: Re: Re: Re: Inspection Report

I am not going to waste my time reading any more of your stupid nonsense. Clean the property or we will terminate the lease - the choice is yours. Do not email me again unless it is of a serious matter.

Peter

From: David Thorne
Date: Friday 02 October 2009 10.36am
To: Peter Williams
Subject: Nom nom nom

Baby Seal

ONE THOUSAND CHARACTERS
POSTING NONSENSE ON THE INTERNET WITHIN PARAMETERS

Tampons

My son's birthday is next week. When he was seven, I told him to draw pictures of what he wanted for his birthday as a visual list, when I enquired as to one image (which I first took to be a box of coloured crayons), I deciphered his explanations as it being tampons. In particular, the multicoloured brand. His only references to the product were the adverts featuring a girl jumping out of a window onto a tree which lowered her into a BMW convertible full of friends, an electric green street racing car with black flames and the ability to do a single-handed handstand star-jump on a dance machine to crowd applause. I bought him a box and figured he would work it out. Yesterday I asked him what he wants for his birthday and he replied 'not tampons'.

Sharks

My son wanted "scuba gear" for his birthday. Thats all he wanted. I am not letting him swim off by himself to be taken for a baby seal by a great white and I will be fucked if I am going in there with him to be taken for an old skinny seal by a great white. When I explained to him that scuba gear is only for the sea and he, being such a small human, would be taken for a baby seal by a great white, he stated that he would see them coming because of the mask and added 'speargun' and 'knife' to his birthday list.

Cats

I promised to look after a friend's cat for the week. My place has a glass atrium that goes through two levels, I have put the cat in there with enough food and water to last the week. I am looking forward to the end of the week. It is just sitting there glaring at me, it doesn't do anything else. I can tell it would like to kill me. If I knew I could get a perfect replacement cat, I would kill this one now and replace it Friday afternoon. As we sit here glaring at each other I have already worked out several ways to kill it.

The simplest would be to drop heavy items on it from the upstairs bedroom although I have enough basic engineering knowledge to assume that I could build some form of 'spear like' projectile device from parts in the downstairs shed. If the atrium was waterproof, the most entertaining would be to flood it with water. It wouldn't have to be that deep, just deeper than the cat. I don't know how long cats can swim but I doubt it would be for a whole week. If it kept the swimming up for too long I could always try dropping things on it as well. I have read that drowning is one of the most peaceful ways to die so really it would be a win-win situation for me and the cat I think.

Girls That Have Said No Part 1

While working at a horse riding camp several years ago, I spent a good twenty minutes explaining to a group which consisted of twelve children and their young teacher, the importance of horse safety before walking behind a horse and being kicked in the head. I recall only walking in a zigag back to the house with the muffled sounds of children screaming in the background before collapsing and waking up in hospital. While I was there, with a fractured skull, the teacher bought me in a get well soon card signed by all the children so I asked her out but she said no.

Riddick

While watching the movie Chronicles of Riddick together last night, my offspring stated that he wished Riddick was his dad. When I asked why, he replied that Riddick is good looking, has muscles and is a good fighter. I told him that I wished Matthew (his arch-enemy at school) was my son because he is better at maths and has cool hair.

Superconductors

If you take the temperature of a superconductor down to absolute zero (around minus 273.1 centigrade), it ignores gravity and floats. This is a scientific fact and you are welcome to check - google or youtube it. My nine year old son asked why we couldn't freeze a car to -273C and fly in it and I told him that the car would neutralise gravity, not reverse it and the weight of the people in it would make it sink. Also, heat rises so -273C should really sink unless it was in a vacuum which means we wouldn't be able to breathe or hear the stereo. You would also need to rug up well.

Girls That Have Said No Part 2

Around the time I was twelve, my sister had really hot friends staying over. I would dress in ninja gear and wriggle 'saving private ryan beach commando style' into her bedroom and listen to their conversations. Some were educational, most were inane. A few months ago, I was standing in a cd store and a girl came up to me and said "Are you David?" to which I replied "It depends" (and immediately regretted as I knew that if she asked me 'depends on what', I had nothing). The fear must have shown because she asked "Depends on what?" and I replied like a retard "On whether it is on or off the record, I have been misquoted by you people before." and she looked at me as if I was a retard before telling me that she had been a friend of my sisters and remembered me and then actually asked "Are you still annoying?" so I asked her if she still "squeezed her nipples while thinking about kissing Michael Wilson". After a pretty long pause I asked her out but she said no.

Anhus Street

A street I drive past every day is called 'Anhus Street' and is very distracting. Every few weeks, someone (I am assuming a kid) spraypaints out the 'h' making it read anus and then a few days later, someone (I am assuming an elderly street resident) paints the 'h' back in. If I was boss of the world I would change that street name legally to Anus Street to annoy both of them.

Girls That Have Said No Part 3

At the local swimming pool canteen, not realising until afterwards that my penis was caught in the elastic of my swimming shorts with the tip sticking out, I purchased a packet of twisties and a can of coke before asking out the girl who served me but she said no.

Parking spot

A few weeks ago, some guy in a shitty BMW parked in my 'reserved and paid for' parking spot in a small lot. I printed out an A4 (Helvetica Demi Bold 12pt) note stating that this was a paid for parking spot and not to park there again. A couple of days later he parked there again. I printed out an A3 (helvetica black 42pt) sign stating 'Reserved Parking, Do not park here' sign and used spray adhesive (3M®) to mount it on the wall in front of my spot. When I went to park in my spot the next day he had written in texta, after "Reserved Parking', the words 'For Wankers'. About three days later I saw his car parked in the street so I printed out a poster in A2 (Helvetica Black, 92pt, reversed) with the word 'Fuckhead' and applied it with spray adhesive to his windscreen, ensuring (as per instructions) I sprayed both materials to be bonded. The disadvantage of course is that I am too scared to park in my spot but he is also too scared to park there so I will class this as a draw for the moment and find a new spot.

Dreams

I hate it when people tell me "I had a weird dream last night...". I dont care, it didn't really happen and it is going to be boring. Just because you dreamt it doesn't make it interesting to anyone. I knew someone who told me a dream and it went on for about twenty minutes. That is nineteen minutes and sixty seconds longer than I have to care about something that didn't really happen. Another time she was telling me about a dream her auntie had, so not only was I listening to something that didn't really happen, I was listening to something that didn't really happen to someone I didn't even know. I glass over and my mind wanders after the words "I had a weird dream last night..." so it is just a waste of everyone's time. The statement she made, "If you cared about me you would be interested in my dreams", I will put down to the fact that she was an idiot and possibly slightly crazy because she owned more than two cats.

My Confession

When I was in year ten, I would wag school to catch the bus into the city. I would hide the contents of my schoolbag and go to a Christian book store called the Open Book, covering two levels and a second hand section in the basement. I would go in with my empty bag, select expensive theological volumes, and fill my bag with several hundred dollars worth. I would then use the toilets to remove any price tags before going downstairs to the basement where they would buy my books for half the retail price. I did this twice a week. I figured that if they caught me I would cry and ask for their forgiveness and as christians they would have let me go but they never caught on. I remember one person buying the entire Amy Grant tape collection when it had been on the shelves not ten minutes before. I was saving for a motorbike and bought a Suzuki Katana. The Open Book went broke a year later so it worked out well for everyone.

Girls That Have Said No Part 4

Around the corner from my place is a 24 hour petrol station thing that I buy what little products I require that don't come in a can (milk) and feed my car (my car is very thirsty and is like having another child in that it is demanding, expensive and problematic. A girl started working there and I thought she was really nice but she would serve me and not speak or make eye contact so I asked her if she had a 'carfor'' and she asked me "what's a carfor" to which I replied "driving around in when I am not paying ninety two dollars to feed it" and she laughed in a very strange manner and went back to what looked like counting in binary in her head. After some small talk (which on hindsight she may have taken as admonishing her on the poor choice of video's they sold), I asked her out but she said no.

Toys'R'Us

Having spent over an hour walking through Toys'R'Us considering gift options for my eight year old offspring, here is a brief list of things I would buy and play with myself if they came in adult sizes;

Ninja costume
Star Wars® Stormtrooper® costume
Remote controlled 'Aerohawk®' twin blade helicopter
Blue Power Ranger® costume
Blow up Wading Pool with palm tree and slippery dip
Electronic Dance Mat for Playstation®
Pink Power Ranger® costume

Girls That Have Said No Part 5

A lady (aged one hundred and ninety) at the counter at Myers in front of me yelled "My purse" then looked at me and proclaimed "You took my purse" so I said "yes, I took your purse, I collect them." and she started yelling at me and the department manager came over and I had to explain that I was not admitting to the theft, I was being sarcastic. Her purse ended up in one of the many bags she was carrying but she continued to glare at me without so much as an apology. When the girl served me she apologised and I asked her "Why, did you arrange someone to act like an old crazy woman for me?" and she laughed and said that I was funny so I asked her out but she said no

eBay

I bought a real dinosaur's tooth fossil recently, with invoice & note of authenticity, as it is something I have always wanted. There is a quarry a short drive away that my nine year old son and I go to and explore sometimes. When we went there last, I suggested we dig for fossils and miraculously 'found' the dinosaur tooth (thinking it would be a big deal to him) but he stated "No, it's just a rock." When I swore I was positive that it is was a 'Saurischian tooth from the Mesozoic era', he replied that I had "made that up" and for me to "throw it away". I cannot prove to him that it is a real dinosaur tooth without divulging the invoice and he is never seeing that as I would have to explain why I didn't buy a playstation 3 instead of a 70 million year old fossil. Occasionally he picks it up and gives me a disdaining look. Also, I bought some NASA mission badges a while back off eBay. He asked me if they had been in space and I had to admit that they hadn't and he stated "Well that's just weak then."

Spiderman 3

I can get by the escaped convict falling into an open air particle accelerator (we have one in the vacant lot next door and I am always telling my 8 year old to stop playing near it), I can even get by the space slime landing coincidently metres from Peter and jumping on his bike... What I cant get past is Mary Jane. What a fucking bitch. In the first movie she is letting the school bully do her, then she lets the rich guy, then Peter has a turn. In the second movie she goes through about eighteen different guys before abandoning her big expensive wedding after realising Peter is Spiderman. In the third film I think she does about sixty guys and whinges a lot about Peter saving lives instead of coming to the theatre to watch her crap acting. Why does he put up with her? It makes no sense and is the one glaring discrepancy in an otherwise completely scientifically believable movie.

Wave Patterns
If a rocket was projected as a wave pattern, setting up harmonics such that they reconstitute the original relationship at another point of space/time, any variations could be sorted by a 'key' included to ensure the reconstruction was identical. If so, a flight to our nearest star, Alpha Centauri, being only four and half light years away would effectively only take 4.5 years. Harmonic travel is impossible and I am making it up as I go along but if we did land on new planets they would definitely have sexy girl aliens. I don't mind if they're green but they would need to not eat me or control my mind.

Ribbons by Sisters of Mercy
Andrew Eldritch used to be too cool for school. I grew my hair for four years to look like him before someone told me I looked ridiculous and more like Edward Scissorhands than him. I first heard the song Ribbons almost twenty years ago while doing 160kmh in a stolen Mercedes down a dark highway on a dark and rainy night. Which would be very cool if it were true, it was actually while riding a horse and listening to a walkman on a sunny day. Which is very not cool. I worked at a horse riding school and had to get up at 5am every morning, break the ice on top of the horses water troughs, feed and then groom the horses. As the riding school catered for school camps, every day I would ride the lead horse on a set path through creeks and hills with five to ten 'follower horses' behind carrying school kids. To make sure the follower horses did nothing but follow, each was fed a blue pill every morning. No matter what the kids did - kick, hit, fall off, the horse would just follow. Because the job was so repetitive, I used to lick the blue pills before giving them to the horses. Apparently I worked there for over a year but I don't remember any of it.

CHIROPRACTORS ARE NOT REAL DOCTORS
I'LL SPEND THE MONEY ON DRUGS INSTEAD

I read recently of a 'qualified' chiropractor that has been using distance healing for quite some time, claiming he can heal you from his living room. There's no need to visit his office, just call or write and he will do the rest. Apparently he discovered his special chiropractic skill while he was in his car, his foot hurt and he told it to realign itself. I did not make this up.

From: Jane Gilles
Date: Wednesday 8 Oct 2008 12.19pm
To: David Thorne
Subject: Overdue account

Dear David,
Our records indicate that your account is overdue by the amount of $233.95. If you have already made this payment please contact us within the next 7 days to confirm payment has been applied to your account and is no longer outstanding.

Yours sincerely, Jane Gilles

From: David Thorne
Date: Wednesday 8 Oct 2008 12.37pm
To: Jane Gilles
Subject: Re: Overdue account

Dear Jane,

I do not have any money so am sending you this drawing I did of a spider instead. I value the drawing at $233.95 so trust that this settles the matter.

Regards, David.

From: Jane Gilles
Date: Thursday 9 Oct 2008 10.07am
To: David Thorne
Subject: Re: Re: Overdue account

Dear David,
Thankyou for contacting us. Unfortunately we are unable to accept drawings as payment and your account remains in arrears of $233.95. Please contact us within the next 7 days to confirm payment has been applied to your account and is no longer outstanding.

Yours sincerely, Jane Gilles

From: David Thorne
Date: Thursday 9 Oct 2008 10.32am
To: Jane Gilles
Subject: Re: Re: Re: Overdue account

Dear Jane,

Can I have my drawing of a spider back then please.

Regards, David.

From: Jane Gilles
Date: Thursday 9 Oct 2008 11.42am
To: David Thorne
Subject: Re: Re: Re: Re: Overdue account

Dear David,
You emailed the drawing to me. Do you want me to email it back to you?

Yours sincerely, Jane Gilles

From: David Thorne
Date: Thursday 9 Oct 2008 11.56am
To: Jane Gilles
Subject: Re: Re: Re: Re: Re: Overdue account

Dear Jane,

Yes please.

Regards, David.

From: Jane Gilles
Date: Thursday 9 Oct 2008 12.14pm
To: David Thorne
Subject: Re: Re: Re: Re: Re: Re: Overdue account

Attached <spider.gif>

From: David Thorne
Date: Friday 10 Oct 2008 09.22am
To: Jane Gilles
Subject: Whose spider is that?

Dear Jane,

Are you sure this drawing of a spider is the one I sent you? This spider only has seven legs and I do not feel I would have made such an elementary mistake when I drew it.

Regards, David.

From: Jane Gilles
Date: Friday 10 Oct 2008 11.03am
To: David Thorne
Subject: Re: Whose spider is that?

Dear David,
Yes it is the same drawing. I copied and pasted it from the email you sent me on the 8th. David your account is still overdue by the amount of $233.95.
Please make this payment as soon as possible.

Yours sincerely, Jane Gilles

From: David Thorne
Date: Friday 10 Oct 2008 11.05am
To: Jane Gilles
Subject: Automated Out of Office Response

Thankyou for contacting me.
I am currently away on leave, traveling through time and will be returning last week.

Regards, David.

From: David Thorne
Date: Friday 10 Oct 2008 11.08am
To: Jane Gilles
Subject: Re: Re: Whose spider is that?

Hello, I am back and have read through your emails and accept that despite missing a leg, that drawing of a spider may indeed be the one I sent you. I realise with hindsight that it is possible you rejected the drawing of a spider due to this obvious limb ommission but did not point it out in an effort to avoid hurting my feelings. As such, I am sending you a revised drawing with the correct number of legs as full payment for any amount outstanding. I trust this will bring the matter to a conclusion.

Regards, David.

From: Jane Gilles
Date: Monday 13 Oct 2008 2.51pm
To: David Thorne
Subject: Re: Re: Re: Whose spider is that?

Dear David,
As I have stated, we do not accept drawings in leiu of money for accounts outstanding. We accept cheque, bank cheque, money order or cash. Please make a payment this week to avoid incurring any additional fees.

Yours sincerely, Jane Gilles

From: David Thorne
Date: Monday 13 Oct 2008 3.17pm
To: Jane Gilles
Subject: Re: Re: Re: Re: Whose spider is that?

I understand and will definitely make a payment this week if I remember. As you have not accepted my second drawing as payment, please return the drawing to me as soon as possible. It was silly of me to assume I could provide you with something of completely no value whatsoever, waste your time and then attach such a large amount to it.

Regards, David.

From: Jane Gilles
Date: Tuesday 14 Oct 2008 11.18am
To: David Thorne
Subject: Re: Re: Re: Re: Re: Whose spider is that?

Attached <spider2.gif>

A Monkey Not sure what kind. If I had a monkey, it would not be like the kind in this picture as this monkey is white and has some kind of fruit smeared all over its face. I would want a clean monkey.

I WISH I HAD A MONKEY

If a woman had sex with a gorilla, getting pregnant and giving birth, we would be able see what man's early ancestors really looked like and include actual photographs in scientific volumes dealing with Neanderthal man. Due to the mixing of species, it might not be possible to produce offspring or it might be more likely if a man had sex with a female gorilla but this would be much less fun to watch. Due to father/mother percentage variations we would probably need about 50 women to do it to get an average. We could put the babies on an island with hidden cameras and see if they invent the wheel and discover fire. Call it Monkey Island and sell series rights. Another bonus would be enough actors to produce footage that would make the opening scenes from *2001 A Space Odyssey* look like a primary school play. I would call mine Manky as it is a cross between man and monkey and would teach him to love.

Obviously having your own monkey would be fantastic for a whole host of reasons but as they are quite intelligent yet unable to speak, they have the advantage of learning very quickly through beatings while being unable to tell anyone. Below is a list of the kind of monkeys that would be good to have. The list is far from complete as it omits Jetski Monkey, Boiling Water Monkey and Battlestar Galactica Monkey but covers the basic best kinds of monkeys.

Disguised Monkey

If I had a monkey, I would borrow my mum's sewing machine and make my monkey a little monkey suit. Then if anyone said "Thats not a real monkey, it's just a monkey suit, I can see the zipper", I could say "I bet you fifty dollars it is a real monkey" and when they said "that seems like a reasonable bet, you are on", my monkey would take off the monkey suit and they would have to pay me fifty dollars. I would buy drugs with the fifty dollars. For the monkey. So he wouldn't mind spending his life in a monkey suit.

Hairdressing Monkey

If I had a monkey, I would teach him how to do my hair - using the appropriate amount of product. I would then set the alarm for him to get up half an hour before I do and do my hair while I am still asleep. This would either give me more time in the morning or allow me to spend more time sleeping. I would just waste the extra half hour anyway so probably better to sleep but as I usually don't rock up to work till ten thirty or so, I could try leaving earlier. This would give me more time to write about what I would do if I had a monkey.

Gambling Monkey
If I had a monkey, I would teach him to count cards like Dustin Hoffman in the movie Rainman and sneak my monkey into the casino. If anyone said "Hey a monkey, whose monkey is that?" I would say "It's not my monkey".

Singing Monkey
If I had a monkey, I would teach it to sing Kylie Minogue songs. Then if Kylie passed out on stage again I would be able to save the day by having my monkey finish the concert for her. The concert promotors would probably give me free tickets and promotional gifts. Kylie would be so thankful that she might send me an autographed photo and I could sell it on eBay for fifty dollars. I would buy drugs with the fifty dollars. Not for the monkey, for me.

Paddling Monkey
If I had a monkey, I would teach it how to use a paddle. The next time I went kayaking I would be able to relax and enjoy the scenery while my monkey navigated the river. Also, the last time I went kayaking I was listening to my iPod and I fell asleep and got sunburnt and the current took me way up the river before I awoke when the kayak hit a tree branch and I had to paddle all the way back. Having a paddling monkey would prevent this ever happening again so really it is a water-safety issue and should be encouraged.

Channel Changing Monkey
If I had a monkey, I would teach it how to use all the entertainment equipment. I would save money on batteries for the remote controls by having my monkey change channels for me. With the money I saved on batteries I would buy drugs. I would share the drugs with the monkey while we watched Black Books and Stephen Chow movies together.

5 Fun Things to do with a Monkey
1. Constructing and flying box kites
2. Eyetoy
3. Running down sand dunes
4. Playing Connect 4
5. Dressups

Surveillance Monkey

If I had a monkey, I would teach it to track down people who annoy me by using their profile photo and google maps. Using earpieces to communicate, I would have my monkey conceal himself behind the person typing on facesook® and when that person wrote something stupid I would have my monkey run up and slap them on the back of the head really hard then make a quick escape. Having several monkeys would be more convenient but I don't have time to train seven monkeys, what with having to do my own hair in the mornings.

Web Monkey

If I had a monkey, I would teach it to download porn for me. This way I could spend my time watching it instead of looking for it. I estimate this would save me one hundred and thirty hours a week. I would obviously require a monkey with similar tastes to mine but how hard can it be to find a monkey with a penchant for pregnant German women in latex?

Yellow Shirt Monkey

If I had a monkey, I would name it Brendon. I would shave the monkey and buy a yellow shirt for it and teach it to write inane posts on the Australian wall. Occasionally I would burn the monkey with a cigarette lighter but not to cause enough damage to detract it from it's primary goal; impersonating a retard.

Ceramic Monkey

If I had a monkey, I would name it Steve Darls and use it for scientific research. I would then publish my findings in a journal titled "Monkey Vs Electricity". With the proceeds from the sale of this publication, I would buy a potters wheel and kiln and produce my own range of contemporary, modern living, statues of monkeys. I could make a cast of my dead monkey and use it to produce to-scale ceramic monkeys. I would design a sticker stating that part proceeds go to Greenpeace but would keep all the money for myself. With the money, I would buy drugs and spend my days stoned, listening to music and
turning pots.

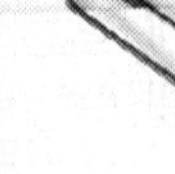

18th May, 2009

Mr David Thorne
[redacted]
[redacted]
Adelaide, South Australia

Dear Mr Thorne,

It has come to our attention through complaints by other tenants in your building that you have a dog at the premises. Under the agreement you signed as part of the Strata, animals are not permitted.

Please call me or email me at hel[redacted]n.com.au to discuss this matter as soon as possible.

Yours Sincerely,

Helen Bailey

STRATA RULES EXIST
FOR THE BENEFIT AND WELLBEING OF ALL RESIDENTS

If I had a large backyard, I would probably have about a thousand dogs but as my apartment is very small, I cannot have any due to both the Strata agreement and the fact that they would need to be taken for walks every day and I am too lazy for that. There is a park across the road from us but the last time I went there I was offered money to provide a sexual act which was kind of flattering but I declined and told them that I was late for a meeting which was a lie as I think I just played Unreal Tournament the rest of that day.

I did have a goldfish named (posthumously) Stinky who lived in a vase with a plant. When he died I figured it would be nice to leave him there so that his body would break down and fertilise the plant but after a few weeks the smell was so bad I could not enter the apartment without a towel wrapped around my face. My first thought was to take him to work and hide him in my Bosses car but out of respect Seb and I gave him a vikings funeral instead.

From: David Thorne
Date: Thursday 21 May 2009 10.16am
To: Helen Bailey
Subject: Pets in the building

Dear Helen,

Thankyou for your letter concerning pets in my apartment. I understand that having dogs in the apartment is a violation of the agreement due to the comfort and wellbeing of my neighbours and I am currently sound-proofing my apartment with egg cartons as I realise my dogs can cause quite a bit of noise. Especially during feeding time when I release live rabbits.

Regards, David.

From: Helen Bailey
Date: Thursday 21 May 2009 11.18am
To: David Thorne
Subject: Re: Pets in the building

Hello David

I have received your email and wish to remind you that the strata agreement states that no animals are allowed in the building regardless of if your apartment is soundproof. How many dogs do you have at the premises?

Helen

From: David Thorne
Date: Thursday 21 May 2009 1.52pm
To: Helen Bailey
Subject: Re: Re: Pets in the building

Dear Helen,

Currently I only have eight dogs but one is expecting puppies and I am very excited by this. I am hoping for a litter of at least ten as this is the number required to participate in dog sled racing. I have read every Jack London novel in preparation and have constructed my own sled from timber I borrowed from the construction site across the road during the night. I have devised a plan which I feel will ensure me taking first place in the next national dog sled championships. For the first year of the puppies' life I intend to say the word "mush" then chase them violently around the apartment while yelling and hitting saucepan lids together. I have estimated that the soundproofing of my apartment should block out at least sixty percent of the noise and the dogs will learn to associate the word mush with great fear so when I yell it on race day, the panic and released adrenaline will spur them on to being winners. I am so confident of this being a foolproof plan that I intend to sell all my furniture the day before the race and bet the proceeds on coming first place.

Regards, David.

From: Helen Bailey
Date: Friday 22 May 2009 9.43am
To: David Thorne
Subject: Re: Re: Re: Pets in the building

David, I am unsure what to make of your email. Do you have pets in the apartment or not?

Helen

From: David Thorne
Date: Friday 22 May 2009 11.27am
To: Helen Bailey
Subject: Re: Re: Re: Re: Pets in the building

Dear Helen,

No. I have a goldfish but due to the air conditioner in my apartment being stuck on a constant two degrees celcius, the water in its bowl is iced over and he has not moved for a while so I do not think he is capable of disturbing the neighbours. The ducks in the bathroom are not mine. The noise which my neighbours possibly mistook for a dog in the apartment is just the looping tape I have of dogs barking which I play at high volume while I am at work to deter potential burglars from breaking in and stealing my tupperware. I need it to keep food fresh. Once I ate leftover chinese that had been kept in an unsealed container and I experienced complete awareness. The next night I tried eating it again but only experienced chest pains and diarrhoea.

Regards, David.

From: Helen Bailey
Date: Friday 22 May 2009 1.46pm
To: David Thorne
Subject: Re: Re: Re: Re: Re: Pets in the building

Hello David

You cannot play sounds of dogs or any noise at a volume that disturbs others. I am sure you can appreciate that these rules are for the benefit of all residents of the building. Fish are fine. You cannot have ducks in the apartment though. If it was small birds that would be ok.

Helen

From: David Thorne
Date: Friday 22 May 2009 2.18pm
To: Helen Bailey
Subject: Re: Re: Re: Re: Re: Re: Pets in the building

Dear Helen,

They are very small ducks.

Regards, David.

From: Helen Bailey
Date: Friday 22 May 2009 4.06pm
To: David Thorne
Subject: Re: Re: Re: Re: Re: Re: Re: Pets in the building

David, under section 4 of the Strata Residency Agreement it states that you cannot have pets. You agreed to these rules when you signed the forms. These rules are set out to benefit everyone in the building including yourself. Do you have a telephone number I can call you on to discuss?

Helen

From: David Thorne
Date: Friday 22 May 2009 5.02pm
To: Helen Bailey
Subject: Re: Re: Re: Re: Re: Re: Re: Re: Pets in the building

Dear Helen,

The ducks will no doubt be flying south for the winter soon so it will not be an issue. It is probably for the best as they are not getting along very well with my seventeen cats anyway.

Regards, David.

From: Helen Bailey
Date: Monday 25 May 2009 9.22am
To: David Thorne
Subject: Re: Re: Re: Re: Re: Re: Re: Re: Re: Pets in the building

David, I am just going to write on the forms that we have investigated and you do not have any pets.

Helen

HELLO, MY NAME IS SHANNON AND I CONSUME AND DIGEST FRUIT LIKE A SNAKE

Due to an extendable jaw and highly acidic saliva levels, I have found that consuming an orange whole and digesting it over the space of many hours, like a snake, requires no effort at all.

I once ate a rockmelon but of course that took many days to digest. People sometimes assume when they see a hint of orange in my mouth that I am wearing a fashionable form of braces or afflicted with a medical condition requiring me to wear a mouthguard at all times - possibly in case of falling over during a seizure or maybe even that sleeping illness you see in movies sometimes. Of course I cannot actually move or do anything while I am digesting but this has not affected my work as I can still move my eyes allowing me to look out the window.

Shannon having lunch

A snake digesting a pig

Blockbuster Video Pty Ltd
555 Portrush Rd Glenunga SA 5064
Tel (08) 8338 0053
Fax (08) 8338 0048
www.blockbuster.com.au
ABN 992 002 682

4.11.2009

Dear Mr Thorne,

I am writing to advise that movies borrowed on the 14th of October are now three weeks overdue and have accumulated fees of $82. Please return the following movies before they gain further fees.

002190382 Journey to the Centre of the Earth
003103119 Logans Run
008629103 Harold and Kumar Escape from Guantanamo Bay
000721082 Waterworld

Kind regards,
Megan

Megan Roberts
Store Manager

Blockbuster Video Pty Ltd
555 Portrush Rd Glenunga SA 5064
Tel (08) 8338 0053
megan.roberts@blockbuster.com.au
www.blockbuster.com.au

DEAR BLOCKBUSTER MEMBER
WE KNOW YOU HAVE OUR DVDS AND WE WANT THEM BACK

I find it annoying to pay late fees on movies and I am too lazy to return them on time which leaves simply complaining about it. I used to know a guy named Matthew who would sell me copies of the latest movies for five dollars each but they were all recorded by someone in a cinema with what appeared to be a low resolution web cam and epilepsy. Several times during each movie the person would shift positions or have people walk past in front and one time filmed the chair in front of him for at least twenty minutes. Matthew's statement was that he did not know the quality before he got them but in one, the person filming answered his phone with "Hello Matthew speaking" and when I mentioned it to him he stopped selling me movies.

From: David Thorne
Date: Sunday 8 November 2009 2.16pm
To: Megan Roberts
Subject: DVDs

Dear Megan,

Thank you for your letter regarding overdue fees. As all four movies were outstanding examples of modern cinematic masterpieces, your assumption that I would wish to retain them in my possession is understandable, but incorrect. Please check your records as these movies were returned, on time, over three weeks ago. I remember specifically driving there and having my offspring run them in due to the fact that I was wearing shorts and did not want the girl behind the counter to see my white hairy legs.

Regards, David.

From: Megan Roberts
Date: Monday 9 November 2009 11.09am
To: David Thorne
Subject: Re: DVDs

Hi David

Our computer system indicates otherwise. Please recheck and get back to me.

Kind regards, Megan

From: David Thorne
Date: Monday 9 November 2009 11.36am
To: Megan Roberts
Subject: Re: Re: DVDs

Dear Megan,

Yes, they are definitely white and hairy. Viewed from the knees down, the similarity to two large albino caterpillars in parallel formation is frightening. People who knew what the word meant might describe them as 'piliferous', although there is something quite sexy about that word so perhaps they wouldn't.

Regards, David.

From: Megan Roberts
Date: Monday 9 November 2009 1.44pm
To: David Thorne
Subject: Re: Re: Re: DVDs

Hi David

No I mean our records indicate that the DVDs have not been returned. Please check and return as soon as possible.

Kind regards, Megan

From: David Thorne
Date: Monday 9 November 2009 4.19pm
To: Megan Roberts
Subject: Re: Re: Re: Re: DVDs

Dear Megan,

With the possible exception of Harold and Kumar Escape from Guantanamo Bay, the movies were not worth watching let alone stealing. In Logan's Run, for example, the computer crashed at the end when presented with conflicting facts and blew up destroying the entire city. When my computer crashes I carry on a little bit and have a cigarette while it is rebooting. I don't have to search through rubble for my loved ones. The same programmers probably designed the Blockbuster 'returned or not' database. Also, while one would assume the title Journey to the Centre of the Earth to be a metaphor, the movie was actually set in the centre of the earth which, being a solid core of iron with temperatures exceeding 4300° Celcius and pressures of 3900 tons per square centimetre, does not seem very likely. Waterworld was actually pretty good though. My favourite bit

was when they were on the water but the scene when Kevin Costner negotiated for peace, ending the war between fish and mankind moments before the whale army attacked was also very good.
Regards, David.

From: Megan Roberts
Date: Tuesday 10 November 2009 3.57pm
To: David Thorne
Subject: Re: Re: Re: Re: Re: DVDs

David

The DVDs are listed as not returned. If you cant locate the DVDs, you will be charged for the replacement cost.

Megan

From: David Thorne
Date: Tuesday 10 November 2009 5.12pm
To: Megan Roberts
Subject: Re: Re: Re: Re: Re: Re: DVDs

Dear Megan,

I have checked pricing at the DVD Warehouse and the cost of replacing your lost movies with new ones is as follows:

Harold and Kumar Escape from Guantanamo Bay $7.95
Waterworld $4.95
Journey to the Centre of the Earth $9.95
Logan's Run $12.95

I have no idea why Logan's Run is the most expensive of the four movies as it was definitely the worst. Have you seen it? I wouldn't pay $12.95 for that. I would use the money to buy a good movie instead. Probably something with Steven Seagal in it. The entire premise comprised of living a utopian and carefree lifestyle with only three drawbacks - wearing seventies jumpsuits, living in what looks like a giant shopping centre and not being allowed to live past thirty. This would seem logical though as I would not want a bunch of old people hanging around complaining about their arthritis while I am trying to relax at the shopping centre in my jumpsuit trying not to think about the computer crashing.

I was recently forced to do volunteer work at an aged care hospital. Footage of these people during Tuesday night line dancing could be used as an advertisement for the Logan's Run solution. The only good aspect of working there was that I halved their medication, pocketing and selling the remainder, explaining the computer listed that as their dose and they were welcome to check knowing their abject fear of anything produced after the eighteenth century would prevent them from doing so. I also swapped my Sanyo fourteen inch portable television for their Panasonic wide screen plasma while they were sleeping, explaining that it had always been that way and their senility was
simply playing up due to the reduced dosage of drugs.
Regards, David.

From: Megan Roberts
Date: Wednesday 11 November 2009 1.21pm
To: David Thorne
Subject: Re: Re: Re: Re: Re: Re: Re: DVDs

Hi David

I have not seen those movies so I dont know what you are talking about. I prefer romantic comedies. If you have the movies we can't rent them so we lose money and the fees are based on what we we would have made from renting them and we also have to purchase movies through our suppliers not from DVD Warehouse.

Megan

From: David Thorne
Date: Wednesday 11 November 2009 3.28pm
To: Megan Roberts
Subject: Re: Re: Re: Re: Re: Re: Re: Re: DVDs

Dear Megan,

I myself am also a huge fan of romantic comedies. Perhaps we could watch one together. I have a new Panasonic wide screen plasma. My favourite romantic comedy is Fatal Instinct although it did not contain enough robots or explosions in my opinion and I was therefore unable to truly identify with the main characters on a personal and emotional level. Recently, I was tricked into watching The Notebook which was about geese. Lots of geese. It also had something to do with an old lady who conveniently lost her memory so she could not remember being a whore throughout the entire film. I don't recall a lot of it as I was too busy being cross about watching it. In a utopian future society she would have been hunted down and killed at thirty.

In regards to the late fees, I understand the amount is based on what you lose by not being able to rent the movies out. You probably had people lined up around the block waiting to rent Logan's Run. For eighty two dollars though, I could have purchased six copies of it from DVD Warehouse or, as I have heard he is a bit strapped for cash, had Kevin Costner visit my house in person and re-enact key scenes from Waterworld in my bathroom.

Regards, David.

From: Megan Roberts
Date: Thursday 12 November 2009 3.16pm
To: David Thorne
Subject: Re: Re: Re: Re: Re: Re: Re: Re: Re: DVDs

Hi David.

Restocking fees are:
002190382 Journey to the Centre of the Earth $9.30
003103119 Logans Run $7.90
008629103 Harold and Kumar Escape from Guantanamo Bay $6.30
000721082 Waterworld $5.70

Total: $29.20 - I have deleted your late fees and noted on the computer that the amount owed is for the replacement movies not fees.

Kind regards,
Megan

From: David Thorne
Date: Thursday 12 November 2009 7.42pm
To: Megan Roberts
Subject: Re: Re: Re: Re: Re: Re: Re: Re: Re: Re: DVDs

Dear Megan,

Those prices seem reasonable. I do not want Logan's Run but will pick up the other three when I come in next.

Regards, David

From: Megan Roberts
Date: Friday 13 November 2009 12.51pm
To: David Thorne
Subject: Re: Re: Re: Re: Re: Re: Re: Re: Re: Re: Re: DVDs

What? The $29.20 is the cost of the replacement DVDs for the store.

Megan

From: David Thorne
Date: Friday 13 November 2009 1.15pm
To: Megan Roberts
Subject: Re: Re: Re: Re: Re: Re: Re: Re: Re: Re: Re: Re: DVDs

Dear Megan,
That makes more sense, I was wondering what I was going to do with two copies of each movie.

Regards, David.

From: Megan Roberts
Date: Friday 13 November 2009 2.33pm
To: David Thorne
Subject: Re: Re: Re: Re: Re: Re: Re: Re: Re: Re: Re: Re: Re: DVDs

What do you mean by two copies? Are you saying you found the four movies?

Megan

From: David Thorne
Date: Friday 13 November 2009 2.57pm
To: Megan Roberts
Subject: Re: Re: Re: Re: Re: Re: Re: Re: Re: Re: Re: Re: Re: Re: DVDs

Dear Megan,

Yes, they were on top of my fridge the whole time. Unfortunately I have a blind spot that prevents me from seeing this area of the kitchen as it is also where I keep my pile of unpaid bills. Last night I slept on the kitchen floor with the fridge door open due to my air conditioner being broken and the temperature outside exceeding that of the centre of the earth. As my fridge emits a high pitched 'beep' every thirty seconds when left open, the vibrations from this caused the DVDs to wriggle forward over the space of many hours before toppling from the edge and I awoke to find them beside me on the pillow. As you have already waived the late fees, I will drop them off tonight and we will call it even.

Regards, David.

From: Megan Roberts
Date: Friday 13 November 2009 3.43pm
To: David Thorne
Subject: Re: Re: Re: Re: Re: Re: Re: Re: Re: Re: Re: Re: Re: Re: Re: DVDs

Ok.

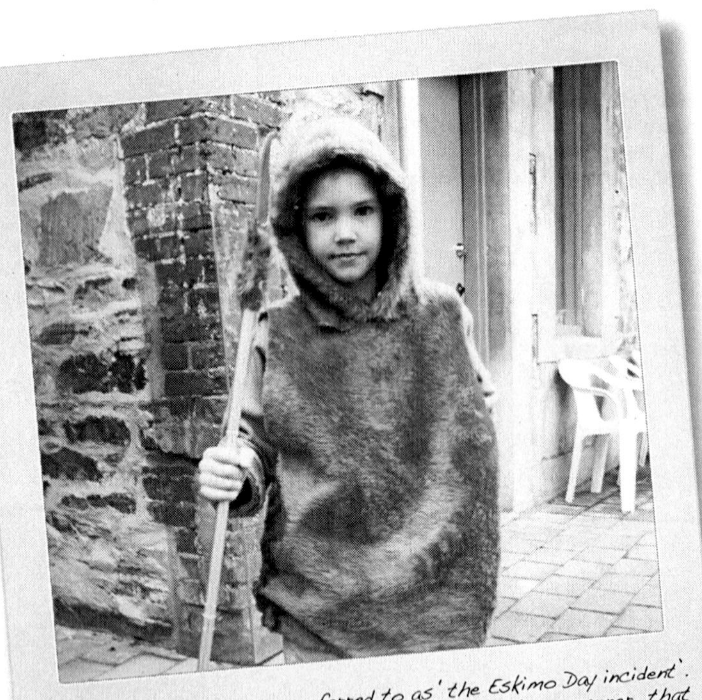

Seb during what is now referred to as 'the Eskimo Day incident'. The school should have explained in a clear manner that 'Eskimo Day' means wearing a warm jacket.

STATEMENTS MY OFFSPRING HAS MADE THAT MAKE ME WONDER IF THERE WAS A HOSPITAL MIXUP

Sometimes I cannot work out my offspring. One moment he will state something that catches me off guard with its clarity, then the next come out with something that causes me to think he may be mentally handicapped.

I was called into his school to speak with the teacher recently. Her statement "He has a good sense of humour but he is the only one that gets it" slightly concerned me but her explanation of why he had received three detentions made me laugh, which is not the reaction she expected:

Detention 1: Raised his hand during maths class and asked "If Kate (a large girl in his class) did not eat for five weeks, would she get skinny or die?"

Detention 2: After teachers had calmed down a very upset child , it was discovered that Seb had told her "I heard the teachers saying that your parents died today and you are going to have to live at the school."

Detention 3: While the principal was explaining the 'no nut policy' due to nut allergies during a school assembly, Seb yelled out "Thats a lot of nuts" after watching the movie Kung Pow the night before.

Money
"If I had a million dollars I would buy a house with big robot legs."

After paying $7.50 for a coffee
"We should open up a shop next to that one, buy their coffees and sell them from our shop for a dollar more."

Our four door Mazda sedan
"We should paint flames on the side. Girls like cars with flames on the side. You will never get a girlfriend in a car that looks like this."

DVD rental prices
"It makes no sense, this one is four dollars for a whole week and this one is six dollars for one night. It is backwards. Someone should tell them."

After being offered a yoghurt sample in a supermarket
"She was nice, you should ask her to be your girlfriend before someone else does."

Paying for petrol
"Leaves burn, why can't we just fill our car up with them? They are free."

On being asked in an elevator what he wants to be when he grows up
"Either a model or a police sniper."

Girls
"You can't trust girls. When I get a girlfriend I am not going to tell her where I live or work."

On being told his minibike had been stolen
"I hope they are riding it and the petrol tank blows up and their legs and arms get blown off and when they are in the hospital they think 'I really wish I hadn't stolen that motorbike'."

The supermarket
"If they made the aisles wider we could drive our car in and grab things through the window and pay on the way out like at McDonalds."

Regarding me being upset over a breakup
"She was ugly and fat anyway, I dont even know how you could kiss her."

Explaining the game Grand Theft Auto 4 to his grandmother
"I don't shoot everybody, just the drug dealers and hookers."

2001 A Space Odyssey
"This movie is so boring. I would rather be staring at the wall and holding my breath for two hours."

Static electricity
"If I am standing on carpet and I get electrocuted, does everybody in the room die apart from me?"

Being told that the park belongs to everybody
"We should buy a fence and make people pay us two dollars to get in."

Relationships
"I am going to have seven girlfriends when I get older so that I can be with a different one every day and then start again on Mondays."

Swimming
"If you swim in the sea then you should always go swimming with a fat girl because sharks will go for them first."

Shoplifting
"If we went into a shop and I put a stereo on and danced, you could run out with a different stereo while everyone is looking at me."

Cleaning
"It will just get messy again. I like it like this, it shows we have better things to do than cleaning."

Marriage
"If you get married, do you have to let your wife look at your penis?"

Super Powers
"If I could have only one super power it would be to breathe in space."

On having homosexuality explained
"That's gross. Not the bit about girls kissing girls though, that's pretty good."

School
"I don't understand why I have to go to school at all, the internet knows more than all the teachers there put together."

Religion
"If I was god I would make all the girls in the world wear no clothes."

Hygiene
"You should never wash your hands because then you will have more germs than everything else and germs won't go on you because there is no room."

Maggie hates Warzone Tower Defence

EDUCATION SHOULD ALWAYS COME SECONDARY TO DISCIPLINE

I do not get on all that well with my son's teacher. Ever since the day she gave him a brochure explaining 'the real meaning of Easter', I have had my eye on her. Recently, my son Seb took a game called Tower Defense to school on his USB drive. I copied it onto there for him. As far as simple games are concerned, I think it is quite strategic and positive. At least it is not about stealing autos and shooting hookers. While I understand taking USB drives to school is a breach of the rules, I do not feel being banned from using school computers is in any way an appropriate punishment. I do however feel a suitable and appropriate punishment for handing out medieval metaphysic propaganda to children would be a good old fashioned stoning.

From: Margaret Bennett
Date: Friday 22 August 2009 3.40pm
To: David Thorne
Subject: computer room

Hello David

I tried to call you but your phone is off. Just letting you know that Seb bought a flash drive to school yesterday and copied a game onto the school computers which is against the school rules and he has been banned from using the computer room for the rest of the term.

Sincerely, Margaret

From: David Thorne
Date: Monday 24 August 2009 9.16am
To: Margaret Bennett
Subject: Re: computer room

Dear Maggie,

Thankyou for your email. I am not answering my mobile phone at the moment due to a few issues with my landlord and neighbours. I am also experiencing iPhone envy and every second spent using my Nokia is like being trapped in a loveless marriage. Where you stay together for the kids. And the kids all have iPhones. I was not aware that my son taking software to school was in breach of school rules. Although the game is strategic and public domain, not to mention that it was I who copied and gave it to him, I agree that banning him from access to the computers at school is an appropriate punishment. Especially considering his enthusiasm for the subject. Also, though physical discipline is no longer administered in the public school system, it would probably be appropriate in this instance if nobody is watching. I know from experience that he can take a punch.

Regards, David.

From: Margaret Bennett
Date: Tuesday 25 August 2009 10.37am
To: David Thorne
Subject: Re: Re: computer room

David

We would never strike a student and whether the software is pirated or not is not the issue. He denied having the drive which means he knew he shouldn't have it here then it was found in his bag so I feel the punishment is suitable.

Margaret

From: David Thorne
Date: Tuesday 25 August 2009 11.04am
To: Margaret Bennett
Subject: Re: Re: Re: computer room

Dear Maggie,

Yes, I agree. Education and access to the tools necessary for such should always come secondary to discipline. When I was young, discipline was an accepted part of each school day. Once, when I coloured outside the lines, I was forced to stand in the playground with a sign around my neck that read 'non-conformist' while the other children pelted me with rubble from the recently torched school library. Apparently a copy of Biggles had been found behind a filing cabinet. Another time, because I desperately wanted a Battlestar Galactica jacket like Apollo in the television series, using brown house paint from the shed at home, I painted my denim jacket and used Araldite to attach brass door hinges as clasps. Feeling that it was an excellent representation and despite the oil based paint still being soaking wet, I wore it to school the next day. Unfortunately, the paint dried while I was sitting in Mrs Bowman's English class, securing me to the chair. After the school handyman cut me free, I was sent to the principal for damaging school property. My punishment was to scrape wads of chewing gum off the bottom of every chair in the school after hours. It took several weeks and it was during this lonely time that I created my imaginary friend Mr Wrigley. During class, when the teacher was not looking, we would pass each other notes regarding the merits of disciplinary action and how one day we would own real Battlestar Galactica jackets. Also, if you happen to see Seb eating anything over the next few weeks, please remove the food from him immediately. He forgot to feed his turtle last week and I feel a month without food will help him understand both the importance of being a responsible pet owner and the effects of malnutrition.

Regards, David.

From: Margaret Bennett
Date: Tuesday 25 August 2009 4.10pm
To: David Thorne
Subject: Re: Re: Re: Re: computer room

David

I hope you are not being serious about the food but I am forwarding your email to the principal as per school policy.

Margaret

From: David Thorne
Date: Wednesday 26 August 2009 11.18am
To: Margaret Bennett
Subject: Re: Re: Re: Re: Re: computer room

Dear Maggie,

Rest assured I would not really withhold nutritional requirements from any child. Except maybe that one that starred in the Home Alone movies. I read somewhere that a healthy breakfast helps concentration and have found, since replacing my usual diet of nicotine with froot loops, I am able to move small objects with my mind. Just this morning Seb and I were discussing the importance of good nutrition which is why, if you check in his school bag, you will find a bag of rice, vegetables, a wok and a camp stove. The gas bottle can be a little tricky but has instructions printed on the side so he should be alright. Please remind him to stand well back and cover his face while igniting as the hose is worn and has developed a small leak.

Also, I am not sure what you are teaching in your classroom but Seb came home the other week talking about a healthy eating pyramid. I had to explain to him that pyramids are made of stone and therefore not edible so I would appreciate you not filling his head with these fanciful notions.

Regards, David.

From: Margaret Bennett
Date: Wednesday 26 August 2009 2.05pm
To: David Thorne
Subject: Re: Re: Re: Re: Re: Re: computer room

David

I have no idea what your point is. I will speak to the principal about the ban but you have to understand that only government approved software is allowed on the computers and Seb knew this rule.

Margaret

From: David Thorne
Date: Wednesday 26 August 2009 2.17pm
To: Margaret Bennett
Subject: Re: Re: Re: Re: Re: Re: Re: computer room

Dear Maggie,

I understand the need for conformity. Without a concise set of rules to follow we would probably all have to resort to common sense. Discipline is the key to conformity and it is important that we learn not to question authority at an early age. Just this week I found a Sue Townsend novel in Seb's bag that I do not believe is on the school approved reading list. Do not concern yourself about it making its way to the school yard though as we attended a community book burning last night. Although one lady tried to ruin the atmosphere with comments regarding Mayan codices and the Alexandrian Libraries, I mentioned to the High Magus that I had overheard her discussing spells to turn the village cow's milk sour and the mob took care of the rest.

Regards, David.

From: Margaret Bennett
Date: Thursday 28 August 2009 11.56am
To: David Thorne
Subject: Re: Re: Re: Re: Re: Re: Re: Re: computer room

David,

I have spoken to the principal and in this instance we will lift the ban.

Margaret

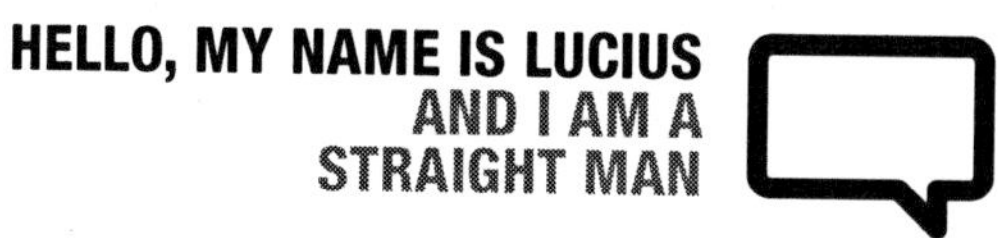

HELLO, MY NAME IS LUCIUS AND I AM A STRAIGHT MAN

I hope this page lets us get to know each other and maybe we can watch football together and other stuff that friends do. But just normal stuff because I am not a gay man.

Starsign
Taurus the lion king.

Favourite colour
All of them. Every colour on our planet is beautiful.

Height
While most females describe me as small, my height is an attribute as I am able to hide in small spaces and everybody loves hobbits. Lord of the Rings was a great movie, it was written by Peter Jackson who also makes cigarettes.

Special skills
I am probably the best at photoshop in the world. If there was a jedi ranking for photoshop skills, I would be a jedi master. Wiggling my mouse with the same dance like grace of a light sabre in the hands of a grand master jedi. Like yoda. But not as tall.

Hobbies
Collecting and swapping unicorn figurines on ebay. I love unicorns, I think it is very sad that we allowed them to become extinct. Man is a selfish animal sometimes. We could have shared the world with them but we hunted them for the magical powers their horns possessed. If I had a unicorn I would meet it in the forest and be gentle with it until the day it trusted me enough to let me ride on its back. Once when I was out dancing, I met some guys who were going to get tattoos so I joined them and got a unicorn on my lower back. It has a rainbow coloured horn which I was told symbolises intelligence and beauty so that is appropriate for me.

Me and my best friend Aaron. Aaron has great tattoos. I was going to get a tattoo but wasn't sure which of my designs was the best. They were all sogreat. Besides, having a tattoo might spoil my chances of getting signed to an international modeling career or something like that.

Aaron giving my skin a close check for discolorations after being out in the sun. He is very sun safety conscious and always makes sure we 'slip slop slap' before going out. He's a great friend and very caring. Nothing gay though because we are both straight.

Mardi Gras I couldnt believe the atmosphere during Mardi Gras – the sound and smell and colourful floats. I wanted to drive one but they wouldn't let me. I would have been a heaps better driver than the guy driving it. I could go heaps faster. I met lots of new friends and had a really good time. Nothing gay though because I am straight and they all knew that.

My favourite Photo of Brad because Brad is showing a sensitive yet cheeky side while still being masculine. If i was gay, which I'm not, i would sleep with Brad. Like if i had to sleep with one man or kidnappers would kill my whole family then i would pick Brad.

Simon D. IKEA spokesperson and web genius

SIMON'S GUIDE TO SHOPPING AT IKEA

Hello, my name is Simon and I love IKEA so much I want to marry it. Can you believe the prices on glass tea light holders? Seventy cents. That is fucking unbelievable. I will get ten.

Here is my simple step by step guide to buying a sofa from IKEA. Some people may think that purchasing a sofa would be a simple exercise but with determination and a little planning, you can ensure that it is a painful process.

Step 1
Ring David at 7.40am and ask him if he will come to IKEA with you. It is important to ring this early as David will be disorientated and agree to anything.

Step 2
Ring David again at 8.05am to check that he got up as getting to IKEA early is imperative. This twenty-five minute interval will ensure that if David did get up, he will be in the shower when you call. Ring David again at 9.15 to enquire where he is and ask him to get you a large latte on the way. If he declines, tell him not to be a selfish prick and remind him of the time you fed his fish while he was away six years ago.

Step 3
When David arrives, inform him that you are taking his car because it is bigger. This is also the time to inform him that you are buying a sofa and he will need to rent a trailer on the way. Now that David is at your place you can get ready at your leisure. As you just put the clothes you want to wear in the dryer, he will have to wait an hour anyway. Make him useful during this time by having him edit a website you are working on about Australian architecture.

Step 4
On the way to IKEA, complain about David's choice in music. Demand a better selection. Make David pull over and tune his stereo to your ipod's itrip and play eighties dance tracks such as 'Big in Japan' by Alphaville loud enough for cars around you to hear. Sing the chorus. If you get the words wrong, explain that's the way they are in another version.

Step 5
When you get to IKEA, do not go straight to the sofa section. Follow the path IKEA has set for you to take and stop and look at every item. Point out the price and comparison of each product by cross referencing it with the IKEA catalogue. Remember to stop at each location point and consult the 'you are here' diagram before progressing. Inform David every two minutes of your exact location in the store by marking your journey on the IKEA map with your IKEA pencil.

Step 6
At the sofa section, sit on every couch and pretend you are watching television. Make David sit next to you like a couple. Also, whenever David is more than five metres away, call out questions such as "What is the foam density of that one?" loud enough for a thirty metre radius to hear. Consult with the staff about every couch. Researching sofas on the internet before you go will enable you to discuss frame warp and fabric weave. Asking about colour choices and availability will involve looking through large sample books. Consult David on each swatch.

Step 7
Once you have made your selection, do not leave the store. Purchase a coffee table and shelf unit and tell David that he will help you put them together when you get home. Also purchase lamps, glass tea light holders, cutlery, ice cube trays, cushions, stackable boxes, an ironing board cover, a quilt cover set and a rug. Make David carry everything, explaining that you need your hands free to write on the IKEA product slip with your IKEA pencil.

Step 8
Before leaving, inform David that you would like to try the famous Swedish Meatballs at the IKEA restaurant. If he states that he will wait in the car, explain that you are shopping together, not one person shopping and the other waiting in the car. Discuss the meatballs on the drive home.

SIMON'S GOOD IDEAS FOR WEBSITES
DO NOT COPY THESE IDEAS AS THEY ARE MINE

Hello, my name is Simon. I have good ideas for websites all the time. Every single one of my ideas would make lots of money.

everything.com
This would be a website where instead of having to look all over the internet for what you want, it would all be in the one place. This would effectively end the need for search engines so I would have to be careful that Google representatives do not kill me in my sleep.

whereaboutsami.com
This would be a website where users can write the name of the city and street they are on and I would tell them where they are.

onlinepetfrog.com
Instead of buying their own pet frog, users would pay a fee and I would buy them a frog and look after it. Users could log on anytime to a live webcam and see how their frog is going and send live requests for me to wave the frog's hand at the camera or bang on the glass if it is sleeping.

whatkindofcoughisthat.com
A website that contains sound files of different coughs. Each cough would have a description to allow the user to sound match and determine the kind of cough they have before going to the chemist and buying either dry or wet cough medicine.

yourloungeroom.com
Users of this website would be able take a photo of their loungeroom and upload it to the site. Then I would tell them what furniture does not look good.

deceasedlovedones.com
This would be a website where you pay a fee to join and are given your own web page with an empty blog. In the event of your death, you can use the page to write a message to your loved ones. Similar setup to prepaid funerals. Your loved ones can either log on and check whether you have left a message for them or can opt to recieve an email notifying them when you leave a message.

howdoigettowhereiam.com
This site would contain a link to the page the user is currently on.

whichonetowear.com
Users of this website would take photos of themselves wearing every combination of every article of clothing they own then upload the images to a user database. Every day, instead of trying on clothing, the user can choose an outfit by simply viewing their choices online.

armbook.com
Similar to facebook but people upload photos of their arms.

everyoneschair.com
A website where you can upload a picture of your chair and then if anyone tries to use your chair and you say "thats my chair" and they say "has it got your name on it" you can send them a link to your photo of the chair which will have the caption 'this is (your name)'s chair'.

screensavingpage.com
A website that is a black page so that people can go there instead of buying a screensaver.

uploadyourscreen.com
A website where the user takes a screenshot of their computer screen and uploads it so that when they are looking at porn and the boss walks past they can type in the link and go to it instead.

picturesofpegs.com
This website would contain pictures of pegs, allowing the user to have access to pictures of pegs whenever they need them.

amihavingaheartattack.com
A website for people having a heart attack.

Pie Chart

Pie I have eaten

Pie I have not yet eaten

SHANNON'S BLANKET OF SECURITY

Due to there being no petty cash left - with which Shannon was planning to buy her lunch - Shannon is now the sole key holder of the petty cash tin, ensuring she never misses out on her lunch again.

Shannon initiates operation "lunch money" with the unveiling of her new Blanket Of Security System (B.O.S.S). The vehicle features internet access for downloading itunes and windows for looking out of.

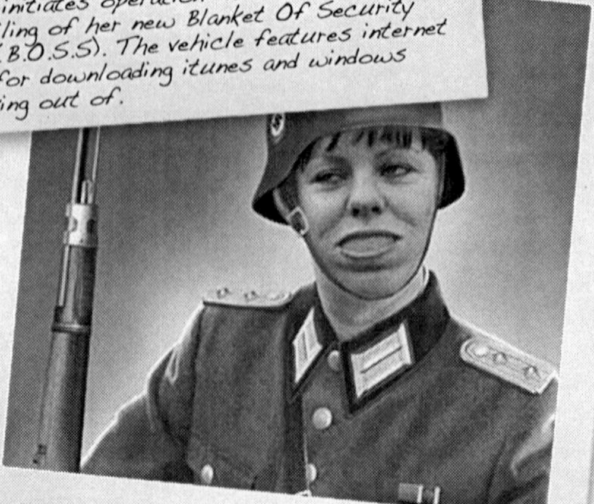

Shannon eating her lunch while keeping an eye on the petty cash tin.

Shannon undercover in petty cash tin stakeout.

Shannon as a young attractive schoolgirl in Nazi Germany circa 1939, looking out of the class window during lunchtime.

Lucius Courier and president of the unicorn hair club

HELLO, MY NAME IS LUCIUS AND I'D LIKE YOU TO SIGN FOR THIS BOX PLEASE AND PRINT YOUR NAME NEXT TO IT. THANKYOU.

Hello, my name is Lucius and I am probably the best courier in the world. If you have a box and you want it to go somewhere, I will come and get it and take it there instead of you having to do it yourself. You have to pay me to do it but it saves you time so it is worth it. It doesn't matter what kind of box, once I delivered a box full of bolts which was really heavy. I am very strong though. They were saying "Wow, that box looks heavy" and I replied "No, it's light for me."

Pickup & Delivery Log

8.30am
The first pick up and delivery of the day is always the best. When I am driving to collect the first box of the day, I try to guess what colour it will be and what will be in it. If the tape on the box is the kind you can lift and put back, I have a look. Sometimes there is food in there. I don't eat it though as that would be against the Courier Code. Once, there was a whole box of sandwiches to be delivered to a work function and they wouldn't have noticed if I had eaten one but I didn't. I took a little bit out of each one but that is allowed.

9.45am
YES! It was a brown box! I knew it would be a brown box. I have definitely got psychotic powers. I have guessed the box would be brown eight hundred and forty times in a row which proves my powers are probably the most powerful in the world. I have to keep my powers a secret though as the government would want to control someone as powerful as I probably am. I would have to live my life on the run, never settling down in one place for long. The government would probably hunt me down and fiifty of them would point their guns at me and I would concentrate and the guns would float up in the air or turn into sticks and the men would say "He is more powerful than we thought possible." I pulled up around the corner to have a look inside the box but it was just books which was disappointing.

10.30am
I delivered the box and the girl in the front foyer signed and printed her name. Her name is Kate and I could tell by the sexy way she signed that she thought I was one of the top five best lookingest guys in Adelaide and

wished I was her boyfriend. I was telling her about my psychotic powers and was going to ask her out but she said she was really busy and had to get back to work. I will see her again later today though as they are a regular client. I will write her a poem in my lunch break. On the way out the door I took a couple of photos of her on my camera phone. She looks a bit surprised in the first photo and blurry in the second as she was getting out of her chair as the door closed. I will use the flash next time. It is somewhere in settings. When anyone has a problem with their phone they always get me to fix it because I am like a computer genius. I am probably the biggest computer genius in the world, I just can't be bothered learning all that stuff.

11.15am
Stuck in traffic on my way to the next box pickup. I feel it might be brown. I like to listen to music while I am waiting and have all the best albums recorded onto TDK Cassette including Arrival, Super Trouper and Warterloo. When I make the final payment on my delivery van in fourteen years, I am going to have a CD Player installed. I saw them at Kmart for only $49.95 so am saving for one. When I am waiting in traffic I turn the music up as loud as it will go and all the rattles in the van vibrate along to it and it is like my van is dancing. Sometimes I become lost in the beat and imagine that I am Paula Abdul dancing with the cartoon cat on the stairs in that music clip where she dances with the cartoon cat on the stairs. I am also probably one of the best singers in the world and when my friend Jedd is in the van I say to him "make me that beat already, so I can destroy it, with my unstoppable flows" and he does.

12.45pm
Eight hundred and forty one! It is a big box too. Priority pickup from one hospital to another. I should not have looked inside that one. I will deliver it after I finish my lunch break and sponge wash. I always keep a wet sponge in the back and I park the van, undress and sponge myself down so that I am clean and refreshed for the rest of the day. I stopped off at Target and bought cologne and a suit, I am going to wear it for Kate. I have also written her a poem:

Kate *by Lucius*

I delivered you a box today
It was brown with clear tape wrapped around it.
I am in the back of my van looking at photos of you
Imagining you opening the box
Wondering what is in it because I didn't look.
The tape was like that when I picked it up.

3.20pm

I have just left the hospital, they were quite rude. A nurse said that she was going to ring my boss and I told her "He might be the boss of me but I am the boss of my life" which was obviously too philosophical for her because she just stood there looking at me. She was completely porned. If I was a transformer she would be so sorry. I took a whole bunch of latex gloves while she was not looking and am on my way to pick up a box to be delivered to the company that Kate works for. I have a strong feeling that this box will be brown and I will drive really fast to get it to her quickly so she sees how professional and efficient I am. I am probably the best driver in the world and if I was a racing car driver I would be world champion.

3.50pm

Eight hundred and forty two! I had to climb six flights of stairs to collect the box but I am very fit and athletic as I own a trampoline and do four hours of air running a night. Air running is where you jump really high then run as fast as you can in the air. It is very good for the vascular system and often my neighbours will come out to watch me. If it was a team sport I would be captain. I am on my way to deliver the box to Kate. I can't wait to see her and I bet she is as excited as I am. I have changed into my suit and put on cologne. I will stand very close to her so that she can smell it. I have cleaned the van up a little bit as I will ask her to come for a ride. Also, I read somewhere that girls like it when you ask them about themselves so in addition to the poem, I have compiled a list of questions for her to fill out about where she lives and what she does.

5.10pm

I am on my way back to the depot as my boss rang and said he needs to see me immediately. Probably to give me a raise or promotion. I delivered the box and Kate absolutely loved her poem, I read it out to her and she was speechless. There were tears in her eyes and she was shaking so I could tell she was overcome with emotion. She couldn't come for a ride in my van because she had a dentist appointment but I could tell she wanted to. She asked me my full name and then repeated it to someone on the phone so I know she feels the same way I do if she is telling her friends about our love. I will buy her lunch tomorrow and surprise her by taking it in and eating it there with her. I will say "special delivery" and when she asks what it is I will say "Me. And a Subway footlong."

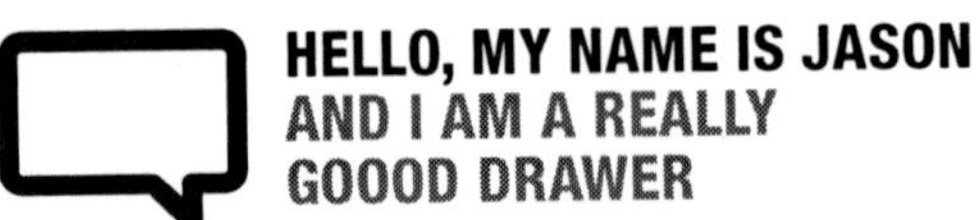

HELLO, MY NAME IS JASON AND I AM A REALLY GOOOD DRAWER

Jason "Hello Sir, my name is Jason and I was wondering if your company would be interested in a good drawer? No? Thankyou for your time."

People often say to me "Jason, you are a good drawer" and I say "Thankyou." To some people, being a good drawer may seem like a hobby rather than a profession but I take it very seriously. Each fortnight, eighteen dollars (ten percent) of my income is spent on conté, charcoal and butchers paper. It is an investment in my future.

Here are some of my drawings. They are all for sale, please contact me immediately if you wish to purchase some of these masterpieces which will no doubt prove to be a very handsome investment.

Name: Whale Looking For Mate
Media: Charcoal on butcher paper
Price: ₿2,800
Name Nina in Floral Dress, Summertime
Media Charcoal on butcher paper
Price ₿5,200
Name: Friendly Tiger
Media: Charcoal on butcher paper
Price: ₿3,000

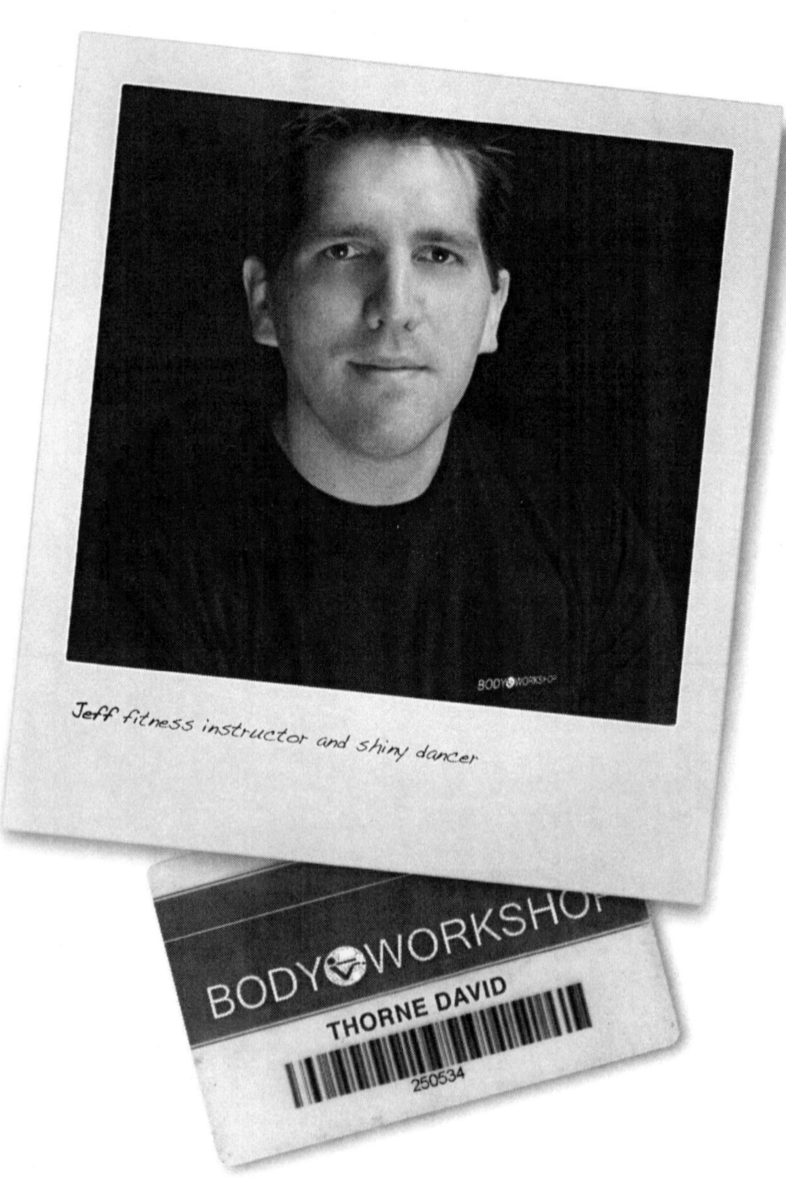
BODY WORKSHOP
Jeff fitness instructor and shiny dancer
BODY WORKSHOP
THORNE DAVID
250534

WORKING OUT WITH JEFF AT TWO HUNDRED AND TEN DOLLARS PER VISIT

I keep telling myself that I should get fit but then I see people that I know and work with starting exercise routines and they become boring and talk about 'reps' and read out the amount of calories from food wrappers as if anybody cares. A year after going to the gym and becoming experts on the amount of water they should drink in a day, they are just as flabby as when they started but less interesting.

As I am constantly told I am too skinny, last year I paid four hundred and twenty dollars to join a gym. I attended twice. The first time for almost an hour, the second for only fifteen minutes when it dawned on me that a) the level of fitness of the people attending the gym was inversely proportional to the level of intelligence and that b) my instructor was not wearing anything under his Spandex bike pants and the wet semen spot would, in all probability, brush against me if I stayed there any longer.

From: Jeff Peters
Date: Wednesday 8 April 2009 10.22am
To: David Thorne
Subject: Membership Renewal

Dear David

This is a friendly reminder to let you know your gym membership expired last week. Your membership is important to us and we would like to take this opportunity to show our appreciation by offering you a 20% discount on your membership renewal. We look forward to seeing you again soon.

All the best, Jeff Peters

From: David Thorne
Date: Wednesday 8 April 2009 1.37pm
To: Jeff Peters
Subject: Re: Membership Renewal

Dear Jeff,

Thankyou for your friendly reminder and the kind offer to reduce my membership by twenty percent. I own a calculator but I could not work out how to do percentages on it so have estimated that I save around $372.10 off the normal price of $420.00 - Please confirm that this is correct and I will renew my membership immediately. Also, do I get a Fitness First sports bag with towel and drinking bottle included in the price? I own my own legwarmers and headband.

Regards, David.

From: Jeff Peters
Date: Thursday 9 April 2009 10.01am
To: David Thorne
Subject: Re: Re: Membership Renewal Due

Hello David

How did you come to that amount? Our half year membership fees are actually $460 but with the 20% discount as an existing member your renewing membership fee would be only $368 for the six months saving you almost $100 off the normal price. We are not Fitness First so do not have those bags.

Cheers, Jeff

From: David Thorne
Date: Thursday 9 April 2009 10.18am
To: Jeff Peters
Subject: Re: Re: Re: Membership Renewal Due

Dear Jeff,

Do I get free shipping with that?

Regards, David.

From: Jeff Peters
Date: Thursday 9 April 2009 12.48pm
To: David Thorne
Subject: Re: Re: Re: Re: Membership Renewal Due

Free shipping with what? The $368 covers your membership fees for six months.

From: David Thorne
Date: Thursday 9 April 2009 2.26pm
To: Jeff Peters
Subject: Re: Re: Re: Re: Re: Membership Renewal Due

Dear Jeff,

By the power of Greyskull that is a lot of money but I admit to being in desperate need of increasing my body strength. My ten year old child often turns the taps off in the bathroom very tightly and I have to go several days without washing. I feel bad constantly having to ask the lady from next door to come over and loosen them for me, what with her arthritis and limited wheelchair access to my apartment. To be honest, I originally joined your gym with full intentions of attending every few days but after waiting in vain for someone to offer me steroids, I began to suspect this was not going to happen and the realisation that I may have to exercise instead was, quite frankly, horrifying. My aversion to work, along with the fact one of your employees, Justin, was rather rude, telling me to "lift this", "push that" dulled my initial enthusiasm of becoming muscular and I stopped attending.

Regards, David.

From: Jeff Peters
Date: Friday 10 April 2009 9.17am
To: David Thorne
Subject: Re: Re: Re: Re: Re: Re: Membership Renewal Due

Hello David

Not sure how to take your email, nobody here would offer you steroids, it is illegal and none of our staff would do this. Justin is one of our most experienced trainers and if you found him rude while he was trying to be helpful and just doing his job then there are plenty of other gyms you could look at joining instead.

Cheers, Jeff

From: David Thorne
Date: Friday 10 April 2009 10.02am
To: Jeff Peters
Subject: Re: Re: Re: Re: Re: Re: Re: Membership Renewal Due

Dear Jeff,

Yes, I have noticed that there are many gyms in my area. I assume the low qualification requirements of fitness trainers means that there is an over supply of these buffed but essentially otherwise purposeless professionals. I knew a guy in high school who couldn't talk very well and collected sticks, he used to call the teacher 'mum' and during recess we would give him money to dance. Then sell him sticks to get our money back. He went on to become a fitness instructor so I view gyms as kind of like those factories that provide a community service by employing people with Down Syndrome to lick stamps and pack boxes. Except with more Spandex obviously.

Regards, David.

From: Jeff Peters
Date: Friday 10 April 2009 10.32am
To: David Thorne
Subject: Re: Re: Re: Re: Re: Re: Re: Re: Membership Renewal Due

Go fuck yourself.

From: David Thorne
Date: Friday 10 April 2009 11.38am
To: Jeff Peters
Subject: Re: Re: Re: Re: Re: Re: Re: Re: Re: Membership Renewal Due

Dear Jeff,

I was, at first, quite surprised at your response; one minute you are inviting me to renew my membership and asking me for money, the next insulting me. After doing a little research however, I have learnt that mood swings are an expected side effect of steroid abuse. As another side effect is a reduction in the size of your penis, this gives you understandable cause to be an angry person. I have also learnt that Spandex contains carcinogenic properties so this does not bode well for yourself and your shiny friends. If I woke up one morning and my penis was a quarter of the size AND I had testicular cancer, I would probably take my anger out on those around me as well. There are probably support groups or websites that could help you manage your problem more effectively and picture based books available on the subject. When I am angry I like to listen to music by Linkin Park. The added angst and desire to cut myself works similarly to the way firefighters fight forest fires by burning off sections, effectively canceling each other out and I find myself at peace. I understand that you guys usually listen to Pet Shop Boys or Frankie Goes to Hollywood but this may be worth a try.

Regards, David.

From: Jeff Peters
Date: Friday 10 April 2009 1.04pm
To: David Thorne
Subject: Re: Re: Re: Re: Re: Re: Re: Re: Re: Re: Membership Renewal Due

DO NOT EMAIL ME AGAIN

From: David Thorne
Date: Friday 10 April 2009 1.15pm
To: Jeff Peters
Subject: Re: Re: Re: Re: Re: Re: Re: Re: Re: Re: Re: Membership Renewal Due

Ok.

From: Jeff Peters
Date: Friday 10 April 2009 1.25pm
To: David Thorne
Subject: Re: Re: Re: Re: Re: Re: Re: Re: Re: Re: Re: Re: Membership Renewal Due

Is that you being a smartarse or agreeing not to email me again?

From: David Thorne
Date: Friday 10 April 2009 1.32pm
To: Jeff Peters
Subject: Re: Re: Re: Re: Re: Re: Re: Re: Re: Re: Re: Re: Re: Membership Renewal Due

The middle one.

LIFESIZE LUCIUS™ CUTOUT DOLL

A while back, I indicated in a certain article that the purchase of a certain T-shirt comes with a free Lifesize Lucius™ doll. Due to having completely made this up, the doll was not delivered with the product so I have provided this page for those who feel hard done by.

Sexy time Lucius. Not just sexy underpants, sexy underpants full of luciusness. Like a boy scout, Lucius is always prepared and knows the best way to bait a trap is with love.

Hell's Angel Lucius. He's a bad boy ladies, playing by his own rules and showing an utter lack of respect for authority apart from the police, road rules and signs.

Shower time Lucius. Scrubbing up and shaving down for a big night out. He's fresh, fragrant and economical due to a single bar of soap lasting several years.

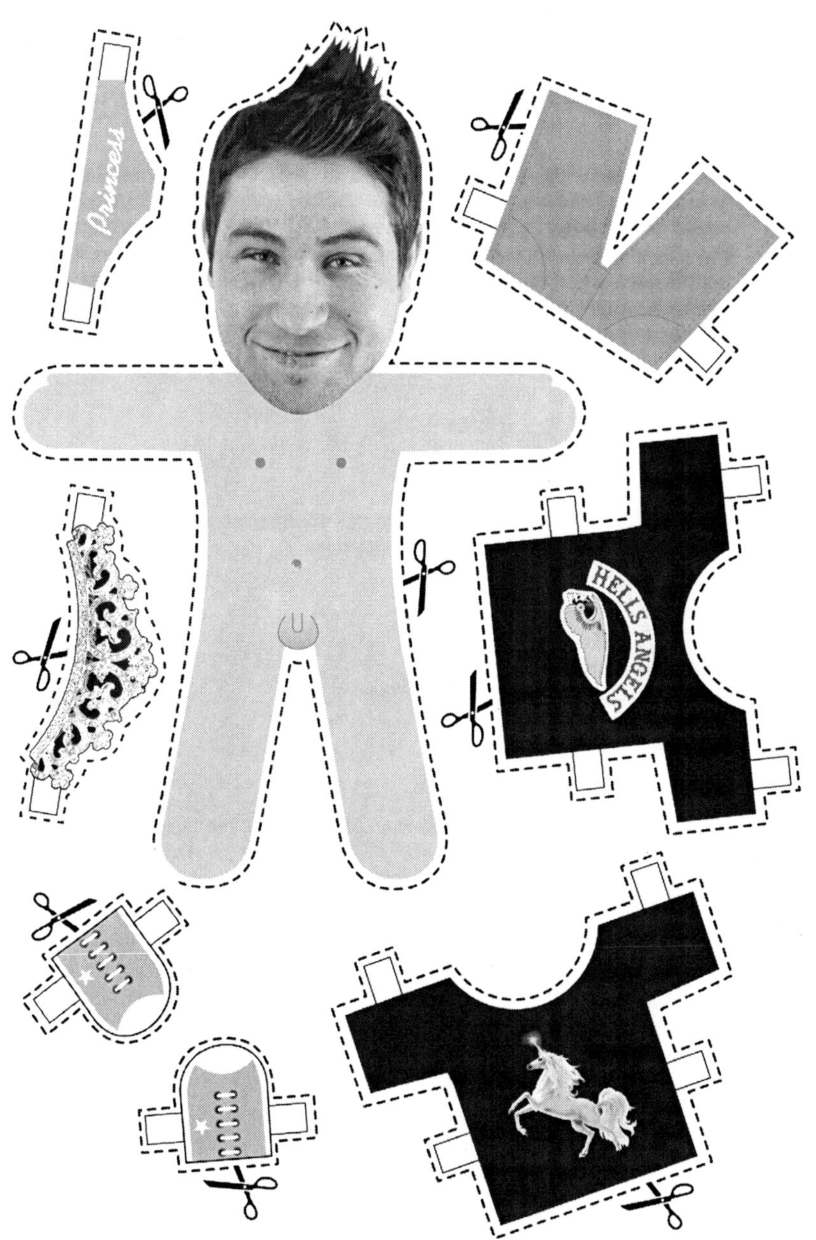
Princess
HELLS ANGELS

SHANNON'S COLOUR CODED COFFEE CUP CLEANING CHART

Due to there being an unprecedented twelve coffee cups needing to be cleaned in the sink at work, it is understandable that Shannon would be outraged by this intrusion on her facebook and looking out the window time. Though kitchen duties may be an expected part of her job role, there is no reason why everyone should not reschedule work/client commitments and help out to ensure Shannon's social networking and looking out the window time is not interrupted.

From: Shannon
Date: Monday 17 August 2009 10.12am
To: Staff
Subject: Coffee cups

There was twelve coffee cups left in the sink this morning. Could everyone please wash their coffee cups after using them.

Thanks, Shan

From: David Thorne
Date: Monday 17 August 2009 10.19am
To: Shannon
Subject: Re: Coffee cups

Morning Shannon,

My apologies. Those coffee cups were mine. I am rather busy today so decided to have all of my coffee breaks at the one time this morning rather than taking twelve separate breaks throughout the day. I am currently experiencing severe heart palpitations but also typing at four hundred and seventy words per minute so should be able to knock off early.

Regards, David.

From: Shannon
Date: Monday 17 August 2009 10.31am
To: David Thorne
Subject: Re: Re: Coffee cups

I was not saying they were all your coffee cups I was just saying that I should not have to wash twelve coffee cups when I don't even drink coffee. People should wash their own coffee cups or at least take it in turns to wash them.

Shan

From: David Thorne
Date: Monday 17 August 2009 10.42am
To: Shannon
Subject: Re: Re: Re: Coffee cups

Shannon,

You raise a valid and not at all uninteresting point. Perhaps you could construct some kind of chart. A roster system would enable us to work in an environment free of dirty coffee cups and put an end to any confusion regarding who the dirty coffee cup responsibility lies with.

David.

From: Shannon
Date: Monday 17 August 2009 1.08pm
To: Staff
Subject: Kitchen Roster

Hi everyone. I have discussed a kitchen roster with David and feel it would be fair if we took it in turns to do the dishes. I have put the roster in the kitchen so everyone can remember. I am Monday morning and Wednesday and Friday afternoon. David is Monday afternoon and Wednesday morning, Lillian is Tuesday morning and Thursday afternoon and Thomas is Tuesday afternoon and Friday morning.

Thanks, Shan

From: David Thorne
Date: Monday 17 August 2009 1.22pm
To: Shannon
Subject: Colour coded coffee cup cleaning chart

Shannon, I notice that you have colour coded the coffee cup cleaning chart. While I appreciate the creative effort that has gone into this roster, the light salmon colour you have chosen for my name is very effeminate. While I am sure you have not done this on purpose and are not inferring anything, I would appreciate you rectifying this immediately. Would it be possible to swap colours with Thomas as he has quite a nice dusty blue.

Thankyou, David

From: Shannon
Date: Monday 17 August 2009 2.17pm
To: Staff
Subject: Updated kitchen roster

Hi. I have changed David's colour to blue on the kitchen roster.
Thomas is now green.

Shan

From: Thomas
Date: Monday 17 August 2009 2.24pm
To: David Thorne
Subject: What the fuck?

What the fuck is this email from Shannon?
I am not doing a fucking kitchen roster. Was this your idea?

From: David Thorne
Date: Monday 17 August 2009 2.38pm
To: Thomas
Cc: Shannon
Subject: Re: What the fuck?

Thomas, do you feel it is fair that Shannon should have to wash everyone's coffee cups? Apparently this morning there were twelve coffee cups in the sink. I was going to schedule a staff board meeting this afternoon to discuss the issue but luckily Shannon has prepared a colour coded coffee cup cleaning chart for us rendering a staff meeting unnecessary. We should all thank Shannon for taking the initiative and creating a system that will empower us to efficiently schedule client meetings and work commitments around our designated coffee cup cleaning duties. If at any stage our rostered coffee cup cleaning commitments coincide with work requirements, we can simply hold the client meeting in the kitchen. We can wash while the clients dry. Today it may only be twelve coffee cups but tomorrow it could be several plates and a spoon and then where would we be?

David.

From: Thomas
Date: Monday 17 August 2009 2.56pm
To: Shannon
Subject: Kitchen stuff

Shannon, I do not need a chart telling me when to wash dishes. I am not going to stop in the middle of writing proposals to wash coffee cups. David is being a fuckwit. I only use one coffee cup and I always rinse it out after I use it. If we have clients here and they use coffee cups then it is appreciated that you wash them as part of your job.

From: Lillian
Date: Monday 17 August 2009 3.06pm
To: Thomas
Subject: Re: Kitchen stuff

What's this kitchen roster thing? Did you agree to this?

From: David Thorne
Date: Monday 17 August 2009 3.09pm
To: Shannon
Subject: Rescheduling coffee cup duties

Shannon, can I swap my rostered coffee cup cleaning duty this afternoon for Thursday? I have been busy all day working, not looking at pictures of Johnny Depp on the internet, and not had time to familiarise myself with correct coffee cup cleaning requirements. I am happy to reschedule my meetings tomorrow to undertake a training session on dish washing detergent location and washcloth procedures with you if you have the time. I feel it would be quite helpful if prior to the training session you prepared some kind of Powerpoint presentation. Possibly with graphs. Will I need to bring my own rubber gloves or will these be provided?

David

From: Shannon
Date: Monday 17 August 2009 3.20pm
To: David Thorne
Subject: Re: Rescheduling coffee cup duties

Whatever.

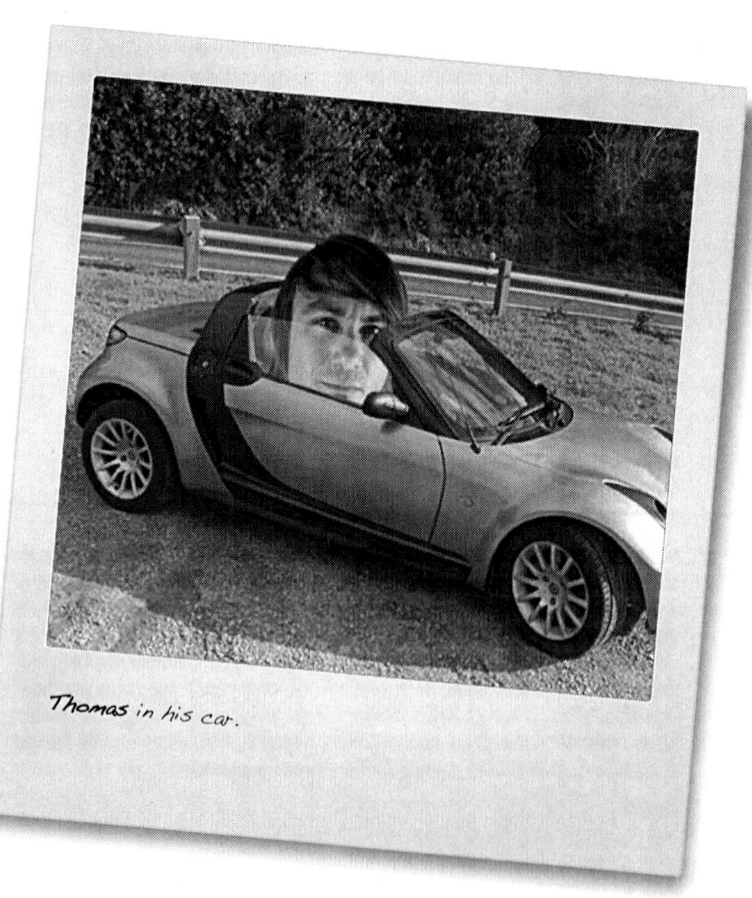

Thomas in his car.

BREAKTHROUGH MEDICAL OPERATION GIVES NEW HOPE FOR THOMAS

It was champagne all round last night in celebration of the medical breakthrough which, despite previous diagnostics, may indeed cure Thomas of the rare condition which has caused his head to swell to unimagined proportions.

Dr Hermine Bergmann is thrilled with the results. “We have been able to reduce the swelling by 85%, bringing his head down to the size of a small family car or large hatchback, similar to the Renault my husband recently bought me” she said. “We have him wearing a two person inflatable boat as a hat to avoid any further damage, but we hope to have his head down to a size where he will be able to drive his convertible with the roof up”.

Thomas’ family are extremely pleased at the breakthrough, “I thought his head was just going to get bigger and bigger till it exploded” said his father, “he’d come over and sit down in front of the telly and noone could see a bloody thing past his great hairy weather balloon of a head. It was fucking incredible, you should have seen it. I would have taken photos but I didn’t have a wide angle lens”.

Medical staff first believed it may have been simply a large tumor with a face but this was disproven when some movement resembling motor skills was observed. “The operation was touch and go there for a while” said Dr Bergmann, “We simply did not have medical instruments designed to cut through that amount of mass, even the industrial laser bought in especially for the operation struggled to get through the eighteen metres of solid limestone, but the patient is doing well now and looking forward to one day being able to wear his trucker hats again”.

Physicists have expressed relief to the news, it was widely considered among the scientific field that Thomas’ head, if allowed to expand further, would develop its own gravitational field affecting planetary rotation.

Flight Commander Thorne of the recent Discovery mission to deliver flannels to the ISS

AN INTERVIEW WITH FLIGHT COMMANDER THORNE

Flight Commander Thorne has been a part of three successful space missions including the recent delivery of new flannels to the international Space Station.

Thankyou for joining us today and congratulations on your recent successful mission aboard Discovery. Could you explain to us what it was like to be in space?

Yes, I can. It was a lot smaller than I expected. I used to try to take in the fact that earth is spinning around a tiny sun which is just one of billions in a tiny cluster that makes up just a bit of our milky way which is one of billions of galaxies with billions of billions of kilometres between them and I would get a massive headache and overwhelming feeling of insignificance with bouts of depression that ultimately led to the breakdown of my third marriage but when you get up there you realise that there is not that much to it.

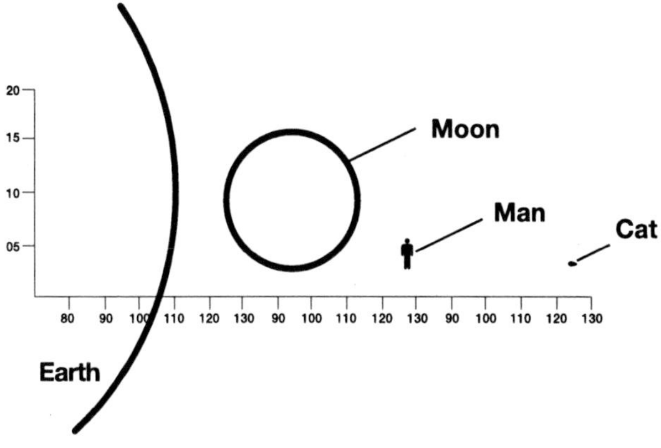

How long does it take to reach your mission destination?

Good question. Contrary to popular belief, distances in space are pretty close, rockets are seriously fast so it only takes about 12 minutes to get to the moon and an hour or so to Mars etc. It was assumed the distances were greater because of our mistaken calculations in regards to the size of objects in space. The moon for example was thought to be 384,633 kilometres away due to the calculation of it having a radius of 3476 kilometres but in fact it is only 16 kilometres up with a radius of

2.3 kilometres. I myself walked the complete circumference of the moon in under an hour and that included stopping often to look at interesting rocks. If I throw one of the rocks out into space it will travel through the void for eternity. I usually do this three or four hundred times each visit. Sometimes I spit on the rocks first, knowing my DNA may travel to another world countless light years away and fertilise a new beginning for mankind.

Could you explain the functions of your suit?

Yes, the suits are pretty cool aren't they. They may look uncomfortable but are actually like wearing a large fluffy quilt and can be put on or taken off in under 30 seconds. I quite often wear mine around the house when I am ironing, mowing the lawn or popping down to the shops to get some milk. The controls on the front may seem complicated but simply control the bass, treble and volume of the built in mp3 player.

How do you prepare for each mission takeoff?

We try to get a good sleep the night before, making sure everything is packed and we haven't forgotten anything. Once the ignition spark hits 20 tons of solid rocket fuel we cant turn around and go to the shop. On one mission, noone remembered to bring cigarettes so the whole trip everyone was bitching and grumpy - I had a packet in my suit but I had to hide them and only smoke in the toilet or everyone would have wanted them. Music is also very important, we strap in, run a pre launch flight check then press the ignition switch hitting us with 9000G of thrust at exactly 12 seconds into the Linkin Park track With You which is fed at full volume through our helmet speakers.

Timeline for Ignition of Booster Rockets

Graph assumes correct volume and bass levels have been set

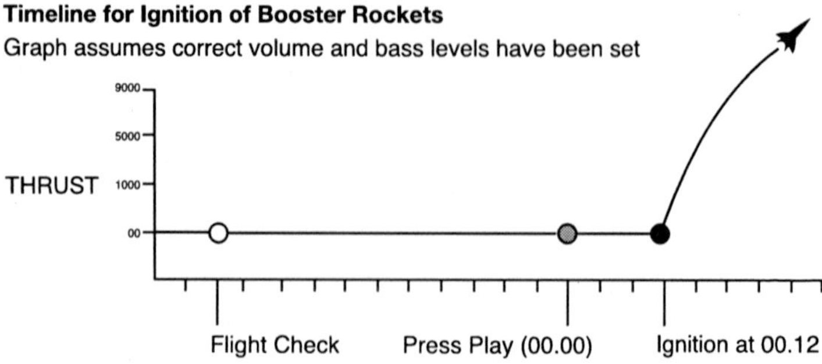

As Commander, you must rely on a dedicated and highly skilled crew to ensure each successful mission.

You would assume that wouldn't you? You would think that a team would support their commander and encourage his leadership and support his decisions wouldn't you. You would expect there to be no bickering about little things or saying stuff behind peoples backs wouldn't you? Good teamwork comes from listening to your commander, that's why there are ranks. Some people just do not understand that there is no I in team. I tell them that the word team stands for Terrifically Exciting Aims Met and had T-Shirts made but they didn't wear them.

Thankyou Commander for taking the time out of your busy schedule to come and talk to us today. Is there any last message you would like to give to our students?

No problem, I wasn't doing much today. Well if there was one message I would like to give to the kids of today, it would be not to do drugs. They may seem fun at the time and yes they may enhance sex and make music sound better but they can be expensive unless you know the right people so you would be better off buying books and pens and stuff. Space may be big but it's nowhere near as big as your potential if you have pens and other writing implements that you may need.

NASA Space Facts

The sun is 20 times brighter than a 60w light globe and generates twice the heat of a potters kiln.

Russian astronaut Mikael Novas has been living on the ISS for 8 years and collects erotica.

You can make your own rocket fuel at home using a 3-1 ratio of chlorine and brake fluid.

Space shuttle Endeavor contains living quarters for 18 people and features a gymnasium and squash courts.

Due to the shuttle taking off in the Florida swamps, several hundred ducks are incinerated during each launch. NASA employees often eat them following a successful take off.

CRAIG'S DOLPHIN COLLECTABLES

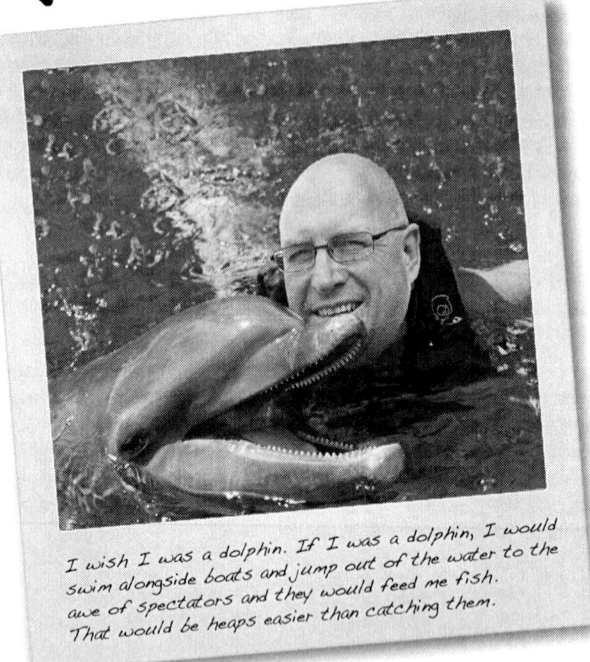

I wish I was a dolphin. If I was a dolphin, I would
swim alongside boats and jump out of the water to the
awe of spectators and they would feed me fish.
That would be heaps easier than catching them.

I love dolphins so much. They are so graceful, sleek, acrobatic, and wet. If I was a dolphin I would be one of those brave ones that fights sharks.

I read somewhere that the dolpin in Flipper was actually several dolphins as the dolphins kept dying. Or it might have been Skippy the kangaroo, I forget which. Either way it is very sad.

Once when I was swimming, I found myself caught in a rip and was carried far out to sea. After several weeks of treading water, I became too weak and gave up hope. As I slipped from the surface and slowly sank like that guy in the movie Titanic, I was rescued by a friendly dolphin who carried me back to his family and fed and nursed me back to health before constructing a small raft out of kelp for me on which I sailed back to shore.

Ever since that day, I have devoted my life to collecting the most beautiful dolphin sculptures in the world. Here are just a few of my favourites:

The most beautiful and magical creatures of the sea, these magnificent dolphins are captured in their wondrous movement atop the crystal waves. As if mirroring the ocean, the waves sparkle with prismatic colors and dazzling lights. I have this on the dashboard of my 4WD, people often remark on its unique beauty. At almost sixty centimetres height it does obstruct some view but is semi-transparent so I do not feel it causes any problem.

In this deliciously decorative delight, a dolphin frolics merrily amongst lacy turquoise reefs. With a charmingly crafted shell for keepsakes, this pleasing scultpture is a dolphin lover's dream! I keep this on my desk at work and use the hanging basket to put my mobile phone in. My ringtone is a dolphin call so everytime my phone rings it is like the dolphin is singing to me. I call this dolphin Carl.

Seashell, dolphins, and coral reef night light. Simply beautiful. If I was a dolphin I would definitely live in an underwater paradise such as this. Leith and I would be the dolphins on the right and the other dolphin would be a friend dropping by. They would remark on what a beautiful home we had and then we would eat that fish.

The only way you sleep through this alarm is if you do it on porpoise. Every morning I wake up to the pleasant sound of dolpin laughs, it makes me chipper, ready for the day and aroused.

One of my favourites, three marbelized dolphins form a cosy nest, awaiting the pleasant aromas which will soon drift from the urn of this absolutely stunning oil warmer. Sometimes I light a candle, add my favourite oil and sit watching it while listening to dolphin calls on my iPod.

A mother dolphin teaches her baby the ways of the sea on this blue-glass carved art piece. With tealight holder. If I was the mother dolphin, I would teach my baby dolphin that life has no set path but that which you choose.

USING THE MATTEL MAGIC 8 BALL™ TO ANSWER EMAILS

I sent an email to a friend recently, asking several different questions, and he replied with the single answer "Yes, probably." It was obvious that he had either not bothered reading the email or could not be bothered answering my questions. The next day I replied to emails by using a Mattel® Magic 8 Ball™ to generate the random answers.

From: Simon
Date: Wednesday 4 Feb 2009 9.38am
To: David Thorne
Subject: No Subject

Have you got a typeface called Garamond Semibold? I have the Garamond and bold and italic but not the semibold. I am doing a poster for Cathy and I reckon garamond would look good.

From: David Thorne
Date: Wednesday 4 Feb 2009 10.02am
To: Simon
Subject: Re: No Subject

As I see it, yes.

From: Simon
Date: Wednesday 4 Feb 2009 10.43am
To: David Thorne
Subject: Garamond

Which one? Yes you have the typeface or that it would look good on a poster?

From: David Thorne
Date: Wednesday 4 Feb 2009 10.52am
To: Simon
Subject: Re: Garamond

Concentrate and ask again.

From: Simon
Date: Wednesday 4 Feb 2009 11.14am
To: David Thorne
Subject: Re: Re: Garamond

What the fuck? I need the typeface Garamond. Have you got it or not?

From: David Thorne
Date: Wednesday 4 Feb 2009 11.18am
To: Simon
Subject: Re: Re: Re: Garamond

You may rely on it.

From: Simon
Date: Wednesday 4 Feb 2009 11.29am
To: David Thorne
Subject: Re: Re: Re: Re: Garamond

Send me the typeface dickhead.

From: Mark Pierce
Date: Wednesday 4 Feb 2009 2.08pm
To: David Thorne
Subject: Hey

Hey. Are you at work?

From: David Thorne
Date: Wednesday 4 Feb 2009 2.25pm
To: Mark Pierce
Subject: Re: Hey

Signs point to yes.

From: Mark Pierce
Date: Wednesday 4 Feb 2009 2.53pm
To: David Thorne
Subject: Re: Re: Hey

What? Can you drop over on your way home from work and help me lift a piece of glass up onto a table? It is too heavy to lift.

From: David Thorne
Date: Wednesday 4 Feb 2009 3.22pm
To: Mark Pierce
Subject: Re: Re: Re: Hey

My sources say no.

From: Mark Pierce
Date: Wednesday 4 Feb 2009 3.49pm
To: David Thorne
Subject: Re: Re: Re: Re: Hey

Are you serious? I tried lifting it a bit at a time and sliding books under it but I need heaps more books. Can you come for a quick drive now?

From: David Thorne
Date: Wednesday 4 Feb 2009 4.02pm
To: Mark Pierce
Subject: Re: Re: Re: Re: Re: Hey

Ask again later.

From: Mark Pierce
Date: Wednesday 4 Feb 2009 4.57pm
To: David Thorne
Subject: ?

Are you going to help me on the way back from work or not?

From: David Thorne
Date: Wednesday 4 Feb 2009 5.16pm
To: Mark Pierce
Subject: Re: ?

It is decidedly so.

From: Mark Pierce
Date: Wednesday 4 Feb 2009 5.24pm
To: David Thorne
Subject: Re: Re: ?

Good. Fuck you are annoying sometimes.

From: Justine Murphy
Date: Wednesday 4 Feb 2009 8.14pm
To: David Thorne
Subject: Tree frogs ppt

Hi David, you forgot to send the attachment on your last email. Can you send it again please?
Justine

From: David Thorne
Date: Wednesday 4 Feb 2009 8.51pm
To: Justine Murphy
Subject: Re: Tree frogs ppt

You may rely on it.

From: Justine Murphy
Date: Wednesday 4 Feb 2009 9.15pm
To: David Thorne
Subject: Re: Re: Tree frogs ppt

Ok. Can you resend it to me then please?

From: David Thorne
Date: Wednesday 4 Feb 2009 9.26pm
To: Justine Murphy
Subject: Re: Re: Re: Tree frogs ppt

Without a doubt.

From: Justine Murphy
Date: Wednesday 4 Feb 2009 9.44pm
To: David Thorne
Subject: Re: Re: Re: Re: Tree frogs ppt

???? Did you attach it?

From: David Thorne
Date: Wednesday 4 Feb 2009 9.51pm
To: Justine Murphy
Subject: Re: Re: Re: Re: Re: Tree frogs ppt

Don't count on it.

From: Justine Murphy
Date: Wednesday 4 Feb 2009 10.27pm
To: David Thorne
Subject: ?

Are you fucking with me? Just attachment it ass hat.

From: Simon
Date: Wednesday 4 Feb 2009 11.28pm
To: David Thorne
Subject: No Subject

Are you online?

From: David Thorne
Date: Wednesday 4 Feb 2009 11.37pm
To: Simon
Subject: Re: No Subject

Concentrate and ask again.

From: Simon
Date: Wednesday 4 Feb 2009 11.41pm
To: David Thorne
Subject: Re: Re: No Subject

Fuck you.

Scott Blog writer and level 47 dwarf

HELLO, MY NAME IS SCOTT
AND I HAVE BEEN WRITING A BLOG FOR EIGHT YEARS

My blog contains the wittiest stuff on the internet. I have had over five hits on my blog during the time it has been running and not all of those have been people I asked to go there.

Because I am a professional blog writer, I recently upgraded my Amstrad CPC 464 to an appropriate system befitting my role. Using my wife's credit card, I purchased fifteen mainframe computer systems but have ordered an additional twenty-five computers as no matter how full my hard drives become, people keep putting new porn on the internet. I have no idea how they expect me to keep up. I feel like Captain Picard commanding the Enterprise when I work and sometimes I wear my Star Trek uniform when my wife is out. My favourite character from Star Trek is Wesley. Once during a freak storm, the electricity in our house went out and I was unable to access my hard drives for over five hours. My testicles grew to the size of small watermelons before rupturing and I was rushed to hospital. While I was recovering in Ward 7G, I made friends with a small boy named Ross in the bed next to me. He died from cancer the next day so I took his Sony PSP.

As a professional blog writer of the wittiest stuff on the internet, I recently decided to quit my job as head assistant chef in charge of pickles at McDonalds and focus full time on my writing career. Due to my unique creative spark and rapier sharp wit, my blog has had unprecedented success and just this week I had another hit. Being a professional blog writer is not all Moët and chicken nuggets though, due to server and hosting fees, I made minus four hundred and ninety dollars last financial year but my wife works three jobs and has a credit card so it all balances out.

If I had friends they would often ask me "Scott, what is the secret behind your champagne quality comedy?" and I would explain to them that it is just a gift and that some people are naturally born with an incredible creative spark while others just get to read it. Recently, I wrote about the time a bee flew in my car window and then flew back out. It was so funny and when I posted a link to it on World of Warcraft, a level 54 dwarf wrote back saying "awesome man" which made my day. Once when I was online in my dwarf clan, I met a level 41 dwarf named Cindy and we fell in love despite her being below my status. I would send her poetry about warcraft and she would edit it for me. As my wife works a hundred and eighty hour week, this gave me plenty of opportunity to organise a liaison with Cindy in real life. After arranging to meet, I packed my dwarf costume and battle axe and used my wife's credit card to buy a bus ticket to the town Cindy lived in. As it turned out, Cindy was actually a real dwarf. And a man. We still made love so as not to waste the money I had spent but I left feeling deceived and only partly satisfied. Why can't people just be honest?

Dividing my time between writing professionally on my blog and online as Scott the Invincible are not my only creative outlets. I am also a professional cartoonist. I am much better than Carl Schultz as my ideas are more clever and creative. I would describe my art as cutting edge with my ears to the street and if you don't get my cartoons then 'yo momma' to you nigga. Here is one of my best cartoons, when I originally posted it my hits went up 400% and all four people said that it was unlike any professional material they had ever seen before.

The cartoon above is funny on two levels which makes it lateral. Firstly, I was looking at porn but said that I wasn't so this is like British comedy and brilliant in itself without the rest. Secondly, I said "make it so" which is what Captain Picard says in Star Trek and I was wearing my Star Trek uniform when I said it. Do you get it? It is probably too clever for you.

If I could give one word of advice to anybody wanting to be a professional blog writer like me, it would be to realise that it does not matter what the subject is, the important thing is how I feel about it. Balance is also important, I find that the best ratio is to have ninety percent of the stories about me and how I feel about things and the remaining ten percent linking to stories about me and how I feel about things.

PAGE ONE HUNDRED AND SEVEN

Hello and welcome to page 107. If you have made it this far by reading the previous 106 pages then I apologise for the fact that it has almost no robots or explosions or exploding robots. If this is not page 107 of the book then my publisher has fucked up somewhere. The fact you are even reading this sentence means the publisher did not proof the manuscript I sent him, otherwise he would have deleted it and sent me an admonishing email. If you simply flicked through and found this page then you have saved yourself a bit of time as there are only about five pages that are vaguely amusing anyway.

My favourite page of the book so far is sixty three, where Richard and Emmeline are shipwrecked on a tropical island and without either the guidance or restrictions of society, emotional feelings and physical changes arise as they reach puberty and fall in love. Later, on page seventy two, where Richard moves with his mother to a neighbourhood in the San Fernando Valley region of Los Angeles, California, their new apartment's handyman, an eccentric but kindly Okinawan immigrant, teaches Richard not only martial arts, but also important life lessons such as balancing on a boat.

Richard Matthews Rove fan.
I
rove.

LOVE LETTERS FROM DICK

I wrote a stupid post a while back about the television host 'Rove' and his dead girlfriend. Basically I asked why no-one mentions his dead girlfriend. Of all the messages I received proclaiming me to be a prick for making statements about his dead girlfriend, Dick's were the most entertaining for me as he just kept going. Unfortunately, I have not received any correspondence from Dick for a while, I will assume he has been arrested by the beard police. This is saddening as it seemed no matter what nonsense I sent him, he would reply in anger.

From: Richard Matthews
Date: Tuesday 6 May 2008 7.42pm
To: David Thorne
Subject: Rove

Fuck you retard wydont you shut up! he dident ask for his gilrfriend to die so use your brain to work out how you would feel and just fucken shutup!

From: David Thorne
Date: Tuesday 6 Nov 2007 8.04pm
To: Richard Matthews
Subject: Re: Rove

Thankyou for your recommendation Dick, I am currently writing a television script that I think you would be perfect for, it features a genius of superior wit and intellect who uses his uncanny abilities to protect the innocent. Aided by his loyal pet, masturbating monkey, he endeavors to right wrongs and solve crimes. At the end of each episode he will leave us with a profound, thought provoking and politically correct statement such as "don't leave your pet in the car with the windows up" or "fuck you retard wydont you shut up." An important part of the character development as I see it, would be the developing relationship between yourself and masturbating monkey. The show will be titled Monkey Dick (a combination of private dick and the pet monkey, similar to Canine Cop) and I do hope you will make yourself available for this opportunity.

From: Richard Matthews
Date: Tuesday 6 May 2008 8.17pm
To: David Thorne
Subject: Re: Re: Rove

Fuck you coksucker you should be ashamed of what you wrote that was wrong ad you know it How wud you feel if you were rove? why dont you fuck off.

From: David Thorne
Date: Tuesday 6 May 2008 8.42pm
To: Richard Matthews
Subject: Re: Re: Re: Rove

You're correct Dick, my statements were uncalled for and unquantifiable in any manner. I apologise without reserve and ask for nothing but your understanding. I hope, in time, you can come to forgive me for such contemptible statements. If I could retract my statements I would but I do not have a time machine. I wish that I did have a time machine, I would take my Macbook Pro back to 1984 and visit Steve Jobs. After selling my laptop to him for millions I would return to the present. I could do this several times as each time the present technologies would have changed. It is a flawless plan, I am sure you will agree, lacking only the availability of time/dimension manipulation technologies.

From: Richard Matthews
Date: Tuesday 6 May 2008 9.02pm
To: David Thorne
Subject: Re: Re: Re: Re: Rove

That didnt even make any sense. why dont you stop wasting your time and get a girlfriend!

From: David Thorne
Date: Tuesday 6 May 200 9.06pm
To: Richard Matthews
Subject: Re: Re: Re: Re: Re: Rove

Thankyou for the excellent suggestion Dick, I contacted your wife and we are now seeing eachother.

From: Richard Matthews
Date: Tuesday 6 May 2008 9.17pm
To: David Thorne
Subject: fuck off

youve obviously got no firends!

From: David Thorne
Date: Tuesday 6 May 2008 9.28pm
To: Richard Matthews
Subject: Re: fuck off

You got me Dick. You are correct, I have no friends. I am lonely and sad. I am currently sitting in a cave by myself, sustaining myself on beetles, powering my laptop by an ingenious array of pulleys and flywheels constructed from small lizards and tree sap from the local flora. I came here to escape my family, friends, industry associates, acquaintances and the lady next door who was spying on me, in the hope of completing my novel titled "why are there so many dickheads messaging me?" I have made the dedication out to you Dick and will endeavor to send you a copy once it goes to print.

From: Richard Matthews
Date: Wednesday 7 May 2008 10.37am
To: David Thorne
Subject: Re: Re: fuck off

Your a moron muthufuka!!!!

From: David Thorne
Date: Wednesday 7 May 2008 11.52am
To: Richard Matthews
Subject: Re: Re: Re: fuck off

Well done Dick, that sentence included a word containing more than three syllables - I am assuming muthafucka to be one word in your dimension. As I mentioned, I am currently writing a novel and would be honored if you would concede to being the editor. I realise that you must be in great demand, with a long list of literary achievements and I am less than worthy of your mastery in this area, but an opportunity such as this could simply not be passed by. I will attach the manuscript and look forward to your positive response.

From: Richard Matthews
Date: Wednesday 7 May 2008 2.18pm
To: David Thorne
Subject: Re: Re: Re: Re: fuck off

youve got mental problems wanker and dont call me dick. your the dickhead!

From: David Thorne
Date: Wednesday 7 May 2008 2.44pm
To: Richard Matthews
Subject: Re: Re: Re: Re: Re: fuck off

Dear Dr Dick,
Thankyou for that in-depth psychoanalysis which is so accurate as to be uncanny. As your professional diagnosis has clearly outlined, I do indeed have mental problems. It is a degenerative disease that causes a small part of my brain to die every time I recieve a message from the kind of person that collects star trek dvds and listens to Jimmy Barnes (yes, I read your profile). Little more can be done except to write a letter to your university, in particular your psychology and psychiatry lecturers, congratulating them on producing such an amazing pool of talent.
Best, David

From: Richard Matthews
Date: Wednesday 7 May 2008 2.52pm
To: David Thorne
Subject: Re: Re: Re: Re: Re: Re: fuck off

fuck you whats wrong with Star Trek? your a wanker

From: David Thorne
Date: Wednesday 7 May 2008 3.19pm
To: Richard Matthews
Subject: Re: Re: Re: Re: Re: Re: Re: fuck off

Nothing is wrong with Star Trek Dick, I enjoy science theory myself and some of the episodes were not completely embarrassing. I was tempted to write something derogatory and perhaps even draw attention to the fact that the only time in any of your emails you have used correct spelling, grammar, punctuation or capitalisation is when you wrote the name Star Trek, but I was fearful that your army of Klingon warriors might attack and shoot colourful laser rays at me, causing me to have to land on a planet inhabited by aliens who speak English and look exactly like humans apart from ripples on their nose while I perform plasma warp drive repairs.

From: Richard Matthews
Date: Thursday 8 May 2008 9.27am
To: David Thorne
Subject: your a wanker

You must be fat and sad and ugly!

From: David Thorne
Date: Thursday 8 May 2008 4.11pm
To: Richard Matthews
Subject: Re: your a wanker

Thankyou Dick, I am touched by your concern for my health, happiness and social acceptance. I actually am not fat and would usually be described as a bit too skinny. I have been contemplating reverse liposuction, a technique where they basically transfer liquified body fat from one patient to another. Having looked on your profile and seen your photo, I was hoping we could help each other out here - I figure some of the fat from just one of your cheeks could help add many kilograms to my current body weight. I realise this would leave you a tad lopsided so if we take the fat from your other cheek we could sell it to the Japanese. This commercial venture would effectively pay for the initial operation and save several whales in the process. I think you will have to agree this is a socially responsible course of action.

In regards to being sad, aren't we all from time to time? As I am sitting writing this on my laptop in bed while my girlfriend watches Family Guy on the 52" plasma screen in her underwear, I cant help but think how much happier I would be if she was Brooke Satchwell, was wearing latex and we were in Bora Bora so I guess happiness being relative and on a comparative scale, you are correct.

As for being ugly, I am actually extremely attractive, with god like features and the body of a Calvin Klein underwear model, due to being born with what is termed the 'drop dead gorgeous gene' but I cant help feeling life would be much easier if I was indeed ugly. Hows it working out for you?

From: Richard Matthews
Date: Thursday 8 May 2008 4.21pm
To: David Thorne
Subject: Re: Re: your a wanker

You think you are fucking clever. I am a primary teacher and the kids in my class write better than you moron! kiss my arse.

From: David Thorne
Date: Thursday 8 May 2008 4.29pm
To: Richard Matthews
Subject: Re: Re: Re: your a wanker

Now I am actually horrified. My son is in primary school and I had the assumption that the adults I leave him in the care of would generally have a higher level of education than his. Just out of interest, can I ask if you have ever had sex with one of your students?

From: Richard Matthews
Date: Thursday 8 May 2008 4.37pm
To: David Thorne
Subject: Re: Re: Re: Re: your a wanker

I teach 3rd grade deadshit

From: David Thorne
Date: Thursday 8 May 2008 4.46pm
To: Richard Matthews
Subject: Re: Re: Re: Re: Re: your a wanker

My question still stands.

From: Richard Matthews
Date: Thursday 8 May 2008 4.58pm
To: David Thorne
Subject: Re: Re: Re: Re: Re: Re: your a wanker

Suck my cock fuckhead

From: David Thorne
Date: Friday 9 May 2008 6.03pm
To: Richard Matthews
Subject: Re: Re: Re: Re: Re: Re: Re: your a wanker

Thankyou Dick, I will take your offer of oral sex as a peace offering but will have to decline. While I appreciate the gesture, I am very much straight. I am flattered and even a little curious but feel it would be better if we refrained from giving in to desire at this stage of our relationship and besides, I would not want to risk doing anything that may damage our friendship - of which I have come to value very much.

From: Richard Matthews
Date: Friday 9 May 2008 11.18pm
To: David Thorne
Subject: Re: Re: Re: Re: Re: Re: Re: Re: your a wanker

what? your an idiot im not gonna compete with an idiot anymore. burn in hell wanker not writing any more to you!

From: David Thorne
Date: Saturday 10 May 2008 1.07pm
To: Richard Matthews
Subject: Re: Re: Re: Re: Re: Re: Re: Re: Re: your a wanker

Compete? I wouldn't attempt such a foolhardy exercise such as competing with a mental giant as yourself. I am possibly the least competitive person I know and am in fact the current national loser in the 'Who is Least Competitive Championships' where trying to win will make you lose. Trying to lose makes you win which makes you lose. Not trying at all makes you lose which makes you win which makes you lose.

From: Richard Matthews
Date: Saturday 10 May 2008 4.40pm
To: David Thorne
Subject: Fucken loser

Yeah your right you do lose. That was the biggest heap of shit i have eva readwhat was that even suposed to mean? dont emai me back you are an idiot.

From: David Thorne
Date: Sunday 11 May 2008 11.13am
To: Richard Matthews
Subject: I love you and want to touch your beard

I am very hurt by your comments Richard and I am not sure quite how to take them. Are you saying it is over? Through time and a series of expensive counseling sessions, I may see my way through it. If you would be interested in perhaps attending some of these sessions together, I believe we may resolve our differences. Its the little things isn't it Dick, the little things that you found cute in the beginning of our relationship have become the catalyst for this anger. I can change Dick. I can change for you. I love you Dick.

From: Richard Matthews
Date: Monday 12 May 2008 10.28am
To: David Thorne
Subject: faggot!

you are a fucken idiot!!! I dont have time to read you stupid shit. What are you even wriing to me for ? I think you are doing it just to annoy me fuckhead

From: David Thorne
Date: Monday 12 May 2008 10.51am
To: Richard Matthews
Subject: Re: faggot!

I confess. You have caught me out Dick, alternative motives may have included 'using dick as entertainment', 'playing with dick' or even 'lets get dick heated' but your super sleuth detective skills have once again outwitted me and centred in on the fundamental reason. Please find attached a cheque made out to you for a copy of your book Detective Dick's Deduction Dictionary. I would also like to sign up to receive your monthly newsletter and please book me in for your course 'Deducing Dick'. If I use my credit card to purchase the full two half hour lessons will I receive the Sherlock Holmes style cap and curved wooden pipe at no added cost? I have my own magnifying glass. Sometimes I use it on ants. Not to cook them, just to warm them on cold days or get a little fire going for them.

From: Richard Matthews
Date: Monday 12 May 2008 11.09am
To: David Thorne
Subject: Re: Re: faggot!

Stop messaging me

From: David Thorne
Date: Monday 12 May 2008 11.22am
To: Richard Matthews
Subject: Re: Re: Re: faggot!

ok

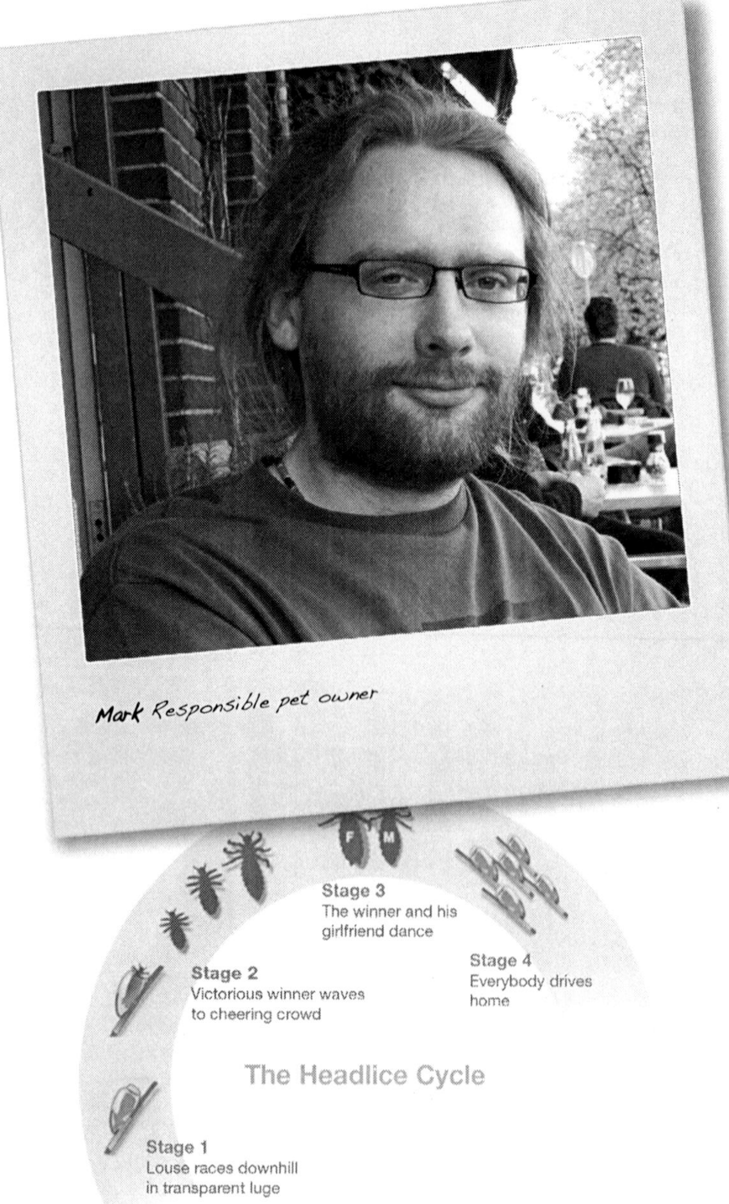
Mark Responsible pet owner
F
M
Stage 3
The winner and his
girlfriend dance
Stage 2
Victorious winner waves
to cheering crowd
Stage 4
Everybody drives
home
The Headlice Cycle
Stage 1
Louse races downhill
in transparent luge

HELLO, MY NAME IS MARK AND I HAVE LICE
SOME PEOPLE FEEL THEY ARE AN AILMENT BUT I ENJOY THE COMPANY

When I was a schoolboy, every month the school nurse would have the children line up for a hair check. Many of my classmates were apprehensive of being found to have headlice but the day the nurse declared "Mark, you have headlice", I felt elated and excited by the idea of living beings choosing me as their provider and calling my hair home. I felt as if I had won a prize. I had never been allowed to have pets at home, my mother, who suffered from a compulsive disorder forcing her to clean, forbade any animals in the house. Unbeknownst to my mother, every night I would water the soil outside my bedroom window and play with the worms that would emerge. That afternoon when I rushed home and told my mother that I had been chosen, her reaction was not that which I had expected and I was forced to wash my hair with KP24, a product designed to kill those that had chosen me. I learned to hate my mother that day and never forgave her. Fifteen years later, on the night she died, I lent over and whispered into her ear that the same product she had used to perform genocide on my headlice was what was in her cup of tea.

Many people feel that headlice are of a sign of dirty or unhealthy hair but this is simply not the case. Like those little fish that live under sharks or those tiny birds that clean alligator teeth, my headlice serve a double role of not only cleaning my scalp but keeping me company. Often, I talk to my headlice or play them tunes on my acoustic guitar. Sometimes when it is very quiet and I concentrate very hard, I think that I can hear them talking to each other and once I am pretty sure I heard my name mentioned.

A few months ago, I was at the hardware store buying a grass trimmer and stopped at the sausage sizzle to purchase a snack. While I was waiting, I bought a raffle ticket that boasted three nights in Bali as first prize. I forgot about the ticket until ast week when I found it in one of my old copies of Nit Weekly while looking for an article I had seen on headlice as an alternative fuel source. I called the number on the ticket and I had won. While I was in Bali, I met a dark skinned native girl and we fell in love. Returning home two nights later, I found that I had pubic lice. I was in the middle of feeding my new friends when my headlice formed a concentrated group and attacked the newcomers leaving every one dead. I believe in protecting me from what they perceived as a threat, they displayed an obvious sign of love.

Another time, when I was canoeing on the river and had to jump out due to seeing a spider in the canoe with me, I forgot I could not swim and was going under when each head lice held onto an individual hair and swam for the surface.

Raising headlice as pets can be a very rewarding experience. Your head-lice will provide you with many years of having something to do with your hands and a great deal of satisfaction knowing you helped to establish and build a community. As their host, it is important to provide them with the neccessities of life. Once a week I give my hair a light spray with chicken stock. In summer I do this daily. On Easter weekend I add a small of amount of chocolate to the mixture and at Christmas time I make them small presents using tweezers and a magnifying glass.

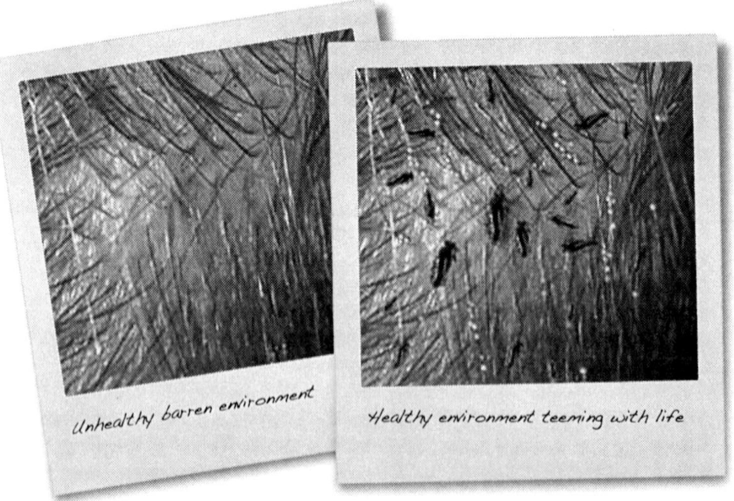

Unhealthy barren environment

Healthy environment teeming with life

I have found with great care, your headlice community will thrive and are even transferable to other parts of your body. I currently have my hair buddies, as I like to call them, living not only on my head but in my eybrows, eylashes and armpits. When I am at the movie theatre, I like to pick headlice out of my hair and place them onto the heads of people in front of me, thus helping my headlice colonise new territories.

Happy Adelaide Folk. Famous for having a silver ball sitting on top of another silver ball and being the highest producer of cannabis and serial killers in the country, Adelaide is only an hour's scenic drive from the capital of Australia, Tasmania.

ROZ LOVES ADELAIDE

Roz Knorr, a pseudonym I will assume unless she is part Klingon, does not like Adelaide. Or perhaps it is just me. Or men in general. She certainly doesn't like my writing and seems to have missed the point that there are plenty of other writers discussing sweat shop children and how man has ravaged Mother Earth. Sometimes it is nice to have a pointless distraction. We can't spend every waking hour kissing trees and throwing paint at women wearing fur coats.

From: Roz Knorr
Date: Monday 12 October 2009 11.56am
To: David Thorne
Subject: Adelaide loser

Only in a backwards town like Adelaide would you get dickheads who would write crap like you. You cant even write well. Thats the result of the sub standard backwards schools in Adelaide. Writing about monkeys and children starving. Spend a few nights with the Salvos feeding the homeless so you can write about that and at least people will go to your site and learn something loser. Little dick typical male. Face it when it comes to Adelaide it is full of dumb backwards hick arseholes that are totally devoid of social consciousness or culture.

From: David Thorne
Date: Monday 12 October 2009 12.38pm
To: Roz Knorr
Subject: Re: Adelaide loser

Dear Roz,
Thankyou for your email. I apologise for the delay in replying. As you mentioned, Adelaide is a tad behind other cities not only in regards to consciousness and culture but also technology. Your email was received by Adelaide's only computer, a 386 housed in the public library powered by a duck on a treadmill, before being relayed to me by Morse code. Should you wish to contact me direct next time, my home number is dot dot dash dot dash dot dot dash.

Regards, David.

From: Roz Knorr
Date: Tuesday 13 October 2009 9.18am
To: David Thorne
Subject: Re: Re: Adelaide loser

Typical coming from such backwards piece of crap city like Adelaide. You just proved my point. LOL! Your reply shows what a bacwards hick you and everyone who lives in Adelaide is. I have homes in Hong Kong, Britain, Paris, USA, & Hawai, as well as Australia. I grew up in a house with 11 servants & a chaufer. And honey I have friends living in Laurel Canyon, & California who earn $400,000 a day in rock & roll. Poor Adeliade. No culture and no class. Be careful not to be a victim of a hit & run. Accidents happen all the time, so much cheaper in Adelaide. One phone call...

From: David Thorne
Date: Tuesday 13 October 2009 9.51am
To: Roz Knorr
Subject: Re: Re: Re: Adelaide loser

Dear Roz,
Thankyou for your concern and kind offer but I should be fine for the moment in regards to monetary based injuries. Recently, I set up a stall at a women's golfing convention with a banner stating "Punch me in the head for one dollar." I made eight hundred and thirty dollars that day. Tax free. With the money raised, I intend to buy a bigger stall for next year's convention. It must be nice to own several homes all over the planet. For many years I dreamt of experiencing the culture of Paris until I realised there would probably be a lot of French people there. They should do something about that. Contrary to your statement regarding Adelaide having no culture though, there is actually a large and thriving artistic community here but very little art is produced due mainly to the artists spending all their time displaying their scarves to each other and attending gallery exhibitions for the free alcohol, food and the chance to wash their armpits in the venue's bathroom.

Regards, David.

From: Roz Knorr
Date: Tuesday 13 October 2009 2.14pm
To: David Thorne
Subject: Re: Re: Re: Re: Adelaide loser

You wouldn't know a thing about culture being from Adelaide. You are a bunch of inbred filthy convicts and are all a bunch of no hoppers. I won't even quote you how much money I make from my busenesses that I have in New York, Britain or Japan.

From: David Thorne
Date: Tuesday 13 October 2009 3.02pm
To: Roz Knorr
Subject: Re: Re: Re: Re: Re: Adelaide loser

Dear Roz,

Actually, while Adelaide may commonly be referred to as the murder capital of Australia due to having more serial killers per capita than any other city in Australia, it is ironically the only Australian capital city not founded by convicts. Adelaide is also referred to as the City of Churches due to the fact that there is a church on every corner. It is not surprising therefore that Adelaide also has a long history of child pedophilia. Another common misconception is that due to Adelaide's high number of churches, the city must be a very religious one. In fact, the number of churches is only necessary in order to cope with the number of funerals as a result of the number of murders that take place here. You are also mistaken in regards to Adelaide containing no hoppers. I myself regularly hop. I am, in fact, the founder of the Adelaide Hopping Club, an organisation that meets each Tuesday to hop. We have so many members that it is often standing room only at the meetings. Which is obviously not a problem. Recently, we have been planning an event in which we intend to hop non stop from Adelaide to Sydney to raise not only awareness for the sport of hopping but also funds for a new charity we have set up called The Roz Knorr Hopping Foundation which will provide poor people with no legs a single artificial leg and accompanying hopping instructional video inspiringly titled 'Never Give Up Hop'.

Regards, David.

From: Roz Knorr
Date: Wednesday 14 October 2009 11.16am
To: David Thorne
Subject: Re: Re: Re: Re: Re: Re: Adelaide loser

You wouldn't know the first thing about charity or giving back to the community. People from Adelaide don't do anything for the underprivileged in society. Go read Naomi Klein's 1999 book "No Logo" and join the ant-globalist movement & start defacing corporate posters in public places with political statements, or visit a sweat shop with 7 year olds in Mexico & blog about it. Until then you are just another selfish parasite taking from this planet. Watch your back. I leave for New York in my private plain this afternoon so I don't have any time for anymore of your pathetic hick town nonsense. Goodbye David.

From: David Thorne
Date: Thursday 15 October 2009 11.55am
To: Roz Knorr
Subject: Re: Re: Re: Re: Re: Re: Re: Adelaide loser

Dear Roz,

Thankyou for excellent suggestions. Unfortunately I cannot afford the airfare to Mexico and even if I did, I do not know any seven year olds to take. It's a pity as I have heard that you can get really cheap soccer balls there. Coincidentally, I too have a private plain. It is actually more of a field but going by the amount of back-packers discovered buried in the area, quite private regardless. I was sitting in the middle of it reading your correspondence regarding poorly written books and eighties political statements when I realised you raise a valid point. I organised a garage sale, in which I sold my neighbours outdoor furniture, and used the proceeds to move to Nimbin. I spent today rubbing my body with crystals, dancing to Fleetwood Mac, writing poetry about rain drops and braiding my leg hair to form rope which I have used to construct dream catchers to sell at the local commune shop. As the commune rejects the concept of money and only accepts happy thoughts in exchange for goods, I am writing this using my laptop powered by karma as an alternative energy source. This email is being sent with an attachment of love.

Regards, David.

From: Roz Knorr
Date: Friday 16 October 2009 10.41am
To: David Thorne
Subject: Re: Re: Re: Re: Re: Re: Re: Re: Adelaide loser

Dangerous ground loser. You do not know who you are dealing with.
I know a lot of people.

From: David Thorne
Date: Friday 16 October 2009 11.09am
To: Roz Knorr
Subject: Re: Re: Re: Re: Re: Re: Re: Re: Re: Adelaide loser

Dear Roz,

Yes, I realise you must know many people, I calculate the six real estate agents, pilot and co-pilot of your private plain, your rock and roll friends making $400,000 a day plus the eleven servants and chauffeur makes a total of twenty two. I am assuming the chauffeur is the person you intend to have me run over by, if not then twenty three. This total does not of course include the people you know from the Salvation Army, ant-globalist movements, sweat shop owners, the shop assistant at your local XXL Golf Pants'R'Us or members of the K.D. Lang Fan Club.

Regards, David.

From: Roz Knorr
Date: Friday 16 October 2009 2.01pm
To: David Thorne
Subject: Re: Re: Re: Re: Re: Re: Re: Re: Re: Re: Adelaide loser

Email me agian and you will be sorry. Bye.

From: David Thorne
Date: Friday 16 October 2009 2.07pm
To: Roz Knorr
Subject: Re: Re: Re: Re: Re: Re: Re: Re: Re: Re: Re: Adelaide loser

▬ ● ● ●   ▬ ● ▬ ▬   ●

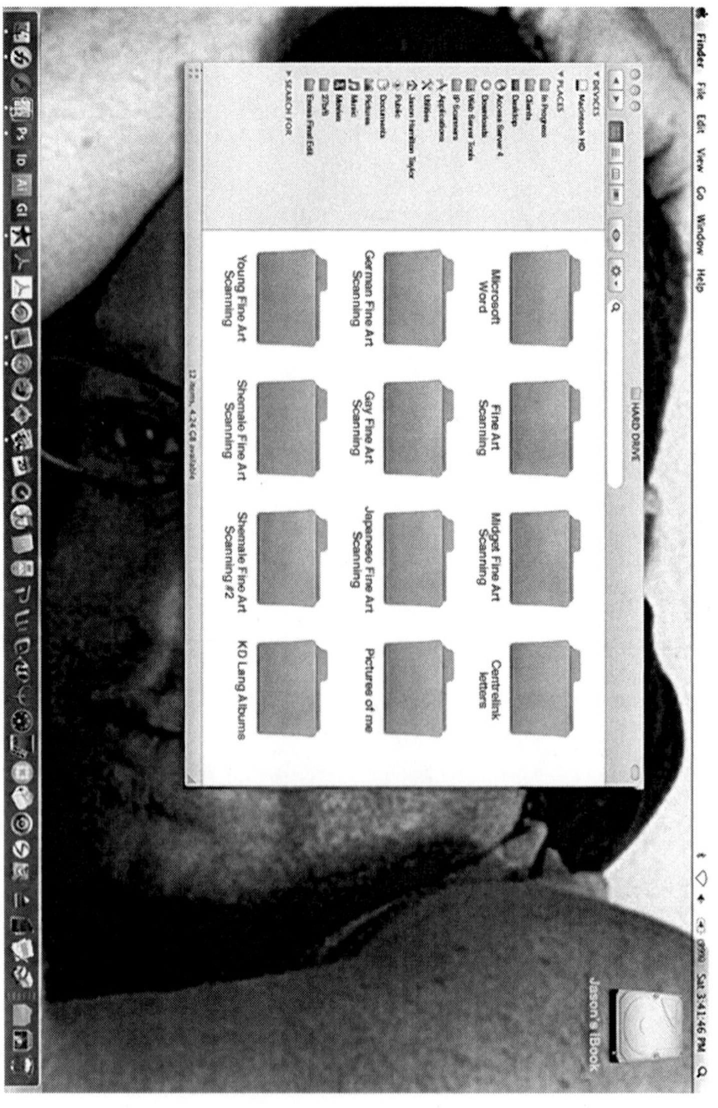
Finder File Edit View Go Window Help
Sat 3:41:46 PM
HARD DRIVE
Microsoft Word
Fine Art Scanning
Midget Fine Art Scanning
Centrelink letters
German Fine Art Scanning
Gay Fine Art Scanning
Japanese Fine Art Scanning
Pictures of me
Young Fine Art Scanning
Shemale Fine Art Scanning
Shemale Fine Art Scanning #2
KD Lang Albums
Jason's iBook

HELLO, MY NAME IS JASON AND I HAVE A MACBOOK PRO. DO YOU HAVE A MACBOOK PRO?

Hello, my name is Jason and I'm creative. I own a MacBook Pro. It's ok if you don't own a MacBook Pro because MacBook Pro's are only for creative people.

Everyone agrees with me that I am the most creative person they know. My MacBook Pro allows me to express my creativity by letting everyone know that I own a MacBook Pro. People sometimes ask "Is that a MacBook Pro?" to which I reply, "Yes it is, because I am creative."

Once when I was hiking and became lost in the wilderness, I was attacked by bears. Luckily, I had my MacBook Pro with me which has my face as the desktop picture. I raised the screen high above my head, effectively looking taller to the bears, and they ran away. I then used the shiny titanium case to signal a rescue plane.

My Apple MacBook Pro

My MacBook Pro is the 12 inch 400mhz version. People are stupid paying so much for the intel Macs. I bought an iBook, painted it silver and used Letraset to write MacBook Pro on it. It is exactly the same as a real one and as I only use Microsoft Word, it suits all my requirements.

Letter to Steve Jobs

Dear Steve,

Thankyou for inventing the MacBook Pro. It is my friend and it is my lover. On the next model, could you please write the word 'Pro' in bold.

P.S. I watched Pirates of Silicon Valley the other night and thought you were a bit mean to your girlfriend. Apart from that you were really cool. I have a poster of you on my wall.

Love Jason

The best thing about having a MacBook Pro is that you can take it anywhere. Now I can have Jason time anytime:

Jason time on the patio with a cold one.

Jason time over coffee.

Jason time curling up in bed.

Jason time relaxing in the bath.

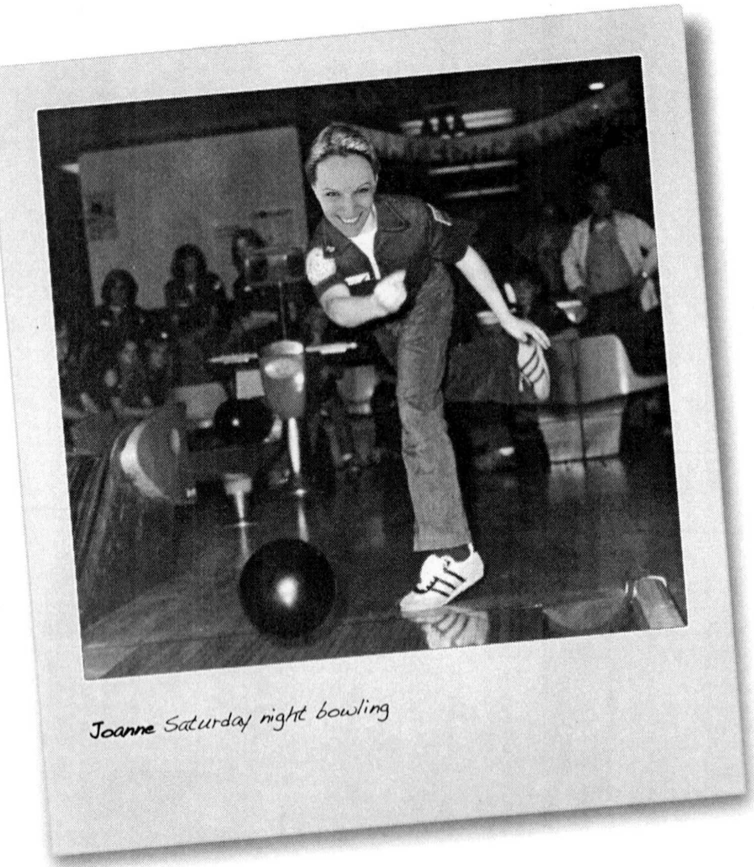
Joanne Saturday night bowling

BARNESYFAN67

Hello, my name is Joanne. My favourite past-time is practicing laughing in the mirror but I also practice dancing so as to be prepared in case I am out and someone puts Bat out of Hell by Meatloaf on the stereo. I also have all the Fleetwood Mac concerts on VHS and have practiced until I have all of Stevie Nicks moves down pat. I dance for my mother sometimes.

I was raised by my two mothers in a large commune whose ideologies incuded balance with nature, meditation and weaving dolls out of straw. When I was nine I was traded to wandering gypsies for six onions. I graduated primary school in my late teens by School of the Air. As we did not own a CB radio, I took all my lessons by tapping morse code onto nearby electrical wires.

I have a poster of a dolphin in my bedroom and have a picture of a tiger on my quilt. I call the tiger Mishka. Sometimes I lie on my quilt and pat him and tell him about my problems. I enjoy sitting in my favourite chair at the window.

My Ideal Partner
I would like to try one with hair this time. It doesn't matter if they don't have all their teeth, I don't either LOL. My last boyfriend Darren had a wicked sound system in his Commodore which was awesome so that would be good. My Datsun has an Audio 4 system that kicks. It has an input plug so that you can play your songs on your iPod through it which is great. I don't own an iPod but if I had a friend with an iPod and they wanted me to drive them somewhere, I would be like "Hey girlfriend, lets play your music on your iPod through my stereo, do you have a N33 adapter cable?" and they would have and we could listen to Keith Urban on the way to Target.

My Ideal Date
Probably something normal like Friday Night Line Dancing at the local pub after a nice meal - either Mcdonalds or Barnacles Bills, I don't mind, I enjoy both red meat and seafood.

Location
I live really close to the train stop which means I can catch the train to the bus stop that takes me to the tram that takes me to a suburb near the

city. Which is really handy because if I knew someone else who lived close to the city we would always be meeting in the city to shop for clothes, drink coffee and talk about Cold Chisel. I have a mobile phone tower in my backyard.

Best Holiday

I'm saving up to go to Bali. Bali is a beautiful and spiritual place and accommodation is very cheap because a lot of villagers drowned to death. Once when I was six my legal guardians took me to the beach and while I was wading, the crab covered corpse of a cruise ship entertainer named Julian washed up on the beach. I hope one of the dead villagers doesn't wash up on the beach while I am relaxing in Bali. Thousands were washed out but I would think that they would have been eaten by crabs and sharks by now which is quite beautiful and spiritual when you think about it. Darren and I used to go crabbing.

Favourite Music

Cold Chisel. I love every album and every song ever released by the Chisels. The Chiz! The depth and, dare I say it, the poetry in Jimmy's musical story telling leaves me breathless. If Jimmy Barnes knew how much I truly understood what he was telling me, he would know that he has found his soul mate and he would get on his Harley Davidson motorcycle and come to my place and we would be lovers. Sometimes when Jimmy is singing, it is like he is talking only to me. My favourite is the track that goes "Kay San, you don't have to put on the red light". If we were on a beach together we would hold hands and spin in circles and laugh like children. If I couldn't marry Jimmy, I would marry Keith Urban and raise wheat on his farm together. Sometimes he would play his guitar and I would sing while I whittled wood.

Favourite Movies

The greatest movie ever made in all time is Pretty Woman. Many people do not get the symbolism in the movie because Julia Roberts did not play her role very well. Sometimes I practice conversations in the mirror and I was in a play once so I would have been much better than her and the relationship between myself and Richard Gere would have been more honest and believable to the viewer. The second best movie ever made is Top Gun. If I had to pick a third best movie ever made, I would have to call it a tie between The Blues Brothers and Dirty Dancing.

Favourite Books

I don't read books but I did once listen to a book on tape called Flowers in the Attic by Virginia Andrews. It was great and reminded me a lot of my own life. Listening to a book on tape is like watching television with the brightness turned down and everyone talking in the same voice but is the whole book in 180 minutes which saves a lot of time. Watching television is heaps better. I own a Teac television because they are the best. My ex boyfriend Darren bought it for me from Cash Converters. It was ninety dollars but he talked them down to seventy five and got two VHS videos with it - Splash and Cannonball Run.

Favourite Television Shows

My favourite show ever was The Young Ones on Channel 2 and I have styled my hair based on the character Neil. Other shows I love are Australian Idol, and Rove. Rove is so funny, I like it when he does other peoples voices, he was a crab in the movie Finding Nemo did you know? It was so sad how his girlfriend died. I once had a boyfriend who I thought died but it turned out he had moved to another suburb with his new girlfriend and thought it would be easier if I was told he had been in a forest fire. Friends is also a great show, everyone on there is just like the friends I would have.

My Poetry

My Gaping Soul *By Joanne*

The sadness and the joy are one. The sadness is a cold, frightened mouse. The joy, a song of life. Like the Bon Jovi song where he is at the Grand Canyon.

Always Being There *By Joanne*

When my boyfriend Darren was working I would ring him every hour to tell him I loved him. I would visit him at his office bi-hourly. True love is always being there. Why did he have to rescue those children from that forest fire?

My Chair *By Joanne*

My chair is near the window. Every day I sit in it. I have venetian blinds so I can see out but people can't see in. If I turn the lights out, I can sit there the whole night and nobody knows I am watching.

Ruffles and Others *By Joanne*

I have a cat named Ruffles. I have more cats but they are referred to as 'others' as I cannot think of eighteen names.

Choices *By Joanne*

The photos on the neon backed menu boards at McDonalds never look like the actual product. Except the apple pie. I will have one of those.

BEES ARE ATTRACTED TO YELLOW
IT IS A SCIENCE FACT

A few months back, while I was meant to be working, I filled out a company's online contact form instead by listing my household furniture and asking what they would give me for it all as trade in on a R1200GS motorcycle.

Several years ago, I did some work for a guy named Andrew who drove to work in a brand new, bright yellow convertible one day. I think it was a Renault. I told him that it is a science fact that bees are attracted to yellow. Being highly allergic to bees, he then refused to drive with the top down, claiming that bees did actually seem to congregate around his car. He would not even drive with the windows down. I think the bees may have simply smelled his fear and approached out of curiosity as I had made the science fact up.

I also sold him a computer stating that it had twice the amount of megatron as other available systems.

Also, in regards to making things up, one of the projects that I worked on for Andrew was a book called Learn to play tennis with Patrick Rafter, possibly the most poorly designed and written book in the history of books. As there was a twelve day deadline for release, which included design, copy and printing time, the text was written on the fly and mostly made up. Though targeted at children, entire pages contain mathematical formulas on calculating the speed of a tennis ball that would confuse NASA scientists.

From: Peter Conner
Date: Friday 9 Jan 2009 09.17am
To: David Thorne
Subject: R 1200 GS

Hello David,
Thankyou for your recent enquiry regarding pricing of the R 1200 GS Motorcycle. We do not accept household furniture as trade ins on vehicles and would reccomend you sell them privately. The R 1200 GS has a list price of $25,470. Please note that this excludes Dealer delivery and ORC and is GST inclusive. I welcome you to contact me personally to arrange a test ride at a time that would suit you.
Sincerely, Peter Conner

From: David Thorne
Date: Friday 9 Jan 2009 10.03am
To: Peter Conner
Subject: Re: R 1200 GS

Dear Peter,

Thankyou for responding to the online request I filled out several months ago and your kind offer to allow me to test ride the product before paying what is essentially five times the value of my car. If you could confirm for me that the model is available in desert yellow I would be very interested.

Regards, David.

From: Peter Conner
Date: Friday 9 Jan 2009 10.22am
To: David Thorne
Subject: R 1200 GS colours available

Hello David,
Yes the R 1200 GS is available in desert yellow. We have a desert yellow demo model on the showroom floor at the moment if you would like to come in to view and arrange a test ride at that time.
Sincerely, Peter Conner

From: David Thorne
Date: Friday 9 Jan 2009 10.48am
To: Peter Conner
Subject: Re: R 1200 GS colours available

Dear Peter,

I have just been informed that bees are attracted to yellow vehicles. Apparently a few years back, a guy I know purchased a bright yellow convertible and was unable to drive it with the top down due to constantly being surrounded by bees. Do you know if this is a science fact? I am allergic to bees and the last thing I want is to be stung in the eye while I am doing 240kph on the freeway during the test ride. Also, do you know if there are airtight motorcycle helmets available?

Regards, David.

From: Peter Conner
Date: Friday 9 Jan 2009 11.09am
To: David Thorne
Subject: Re: Re: R 1200 GS colours available

Hello David,
You would be required to follow state speed restrictions of 100kph on the Eastern Freeway during a test ride and would reccomend lower speeds than that until you have familiarised yourself with the bike. We would generally not expect people to take the demo bike on the freeway but we can discuss when you come in. I have never heard that about bees liking yellow vehicles and would think it is not true. The R 1200 GS is available in granite, black and red in addition to the yellow. Would you like to come in today and discus?
Sincerely, Peter Conner

From: David Thorne
Date: Friday 9 Jan 2009 02.50pm
To: Peter Conner
Subject: Re: Re: Re: R 1200 GS colours available

Dear Peter,

I have been researching bees on the internet for the last four hours at work. When I type "Do bees like yellow" into google, it states that there are 2,960,000 results. It will take me a while to look at that many pages so I doubt I will make it in there today. One of the pages states that Qantas once had a yellow kangaroo as their logo but when it was painted on the tail fin it attracted nests of bees so the logo was changed to red in the mid fifties. This would seem to support the argument that bees are indeed attracted to yellow and contradicts what you have told me. Admittedly though, another page states that bees are technically unable to fly due to their wings being too small for their body weight but I have seen them doing it so this can't be true - somebody should check the internet and make sure everything on there is correct. Regardless, I do not think having to dodge bees in addition to the already present dangers of learning to ride a motorbike for the first time would be very safe. Once when I was a passenger in a yellow taxi, a bee flew in and I screamed causing the driver to swerve and hit a wheelie bin. I will continue my research and confirm that this would not be a factor before I arrange the test ride.

Regards, David.

From: Peter Conner
Date: Friday 9 Jan 2009 03.18pm
To: David Thorne
Subject: Re: Re: Re: Re: R 1200 GS colours available

When you say you are learning to ride a motorcycle, do you hold a current full motorcycle license?
Sincerely, Peter Conner

From: David Thorne
Date: Friday 9 Jan 2009 03.40pm
To: Peter Conner
Subject: Re: Re: Re: Re: Re: R 1200 GS colours available

Dear Peter,

No, but how hard can it be? They are just pushbikes with engines. Part of my daily job role is to ride to collect co-workers lunch orders from McDonalds. I balance the bags on my handlebars because they will not buy me a basket. I think that qualifies me for something. Often, I have to make the trip twice when McDonalds® employees leave something out of the order. Actually, on average, every third time I go through the drive through they forget to include prt of my order. Also the girls who work there are too attractive. This means that if I want something from my local McDonalds® late at night, I have to shower, shave and wear something nice before I can get a simple snack. As it takes me at least two hours to do my hair, I am practically starving by this time and therefore order twice as much food as usual. Ordering more food increases the chance of them leaving something out. Last night it was an apple pie and that is really the only thing I like from there. It is quite obvious to me that they do this on purpose. Once, I ordered two big macs, minus the beef, large fries and an apple pie. When I got home and opened the bag, there were two happy meals in there. The toy in each was a Kim Possible figurine which worked out well as I gave one to my son and kept one myself. For a cartoon character, you have to admit that Kim Possible is quite attractive. I also have a thing for Lois from the television series Family Guy so I must have a penchant for cartoon redheads which is vaguely puzzling to me as I cannot stand redheads in real life. Nobody can. I read somewhere that redheads are more prone to allergies and if this is a science fact, and includes allergies to bee stings, all redheads should be encouraged to wear bright yellow T-Shirts.

Regards, David.

From: Peter Conner
Date: Friday 9 Jan 2009 04.28pm
To: David Thorne
Subject: R 1200 GS test ride

Dear David,
I apologise but we will be unable to organise a test ride for you at this time.
Sincerely, Peter Conner

TOM THE SAD CAVEMAN

John & his bicycle which is made of a titanium composite alloy such as NASA uses on the space shuttle and it has Shimano gears which are the best.

HELLO, MY NAME IS JOHN AND MY BICYCLE HAS A TITANIUM ALLOY FRAME SUCH AS NASA USES

Every weekend and most weekdays, I ride my bicycle to the local cafe to meet other people who ride bicycles and we drink coffee and talk about bicycles.

Riding a bicycle has many advantages. As you do not have to register bicycles or obey any road rules, I am currently constructing a four person family bicycle which consists of two bicycles welded together with four armchairs in between. Due to the extra weight, I have added an engine and am devising a roof, doors and storage area at the back allowing us to ride in all weather conditions and take it shopping.

Sometimes when I am riding my bicycle I feel like I am the only person on the road. If I have my earphones in and the iPod turned up really loud, I cannot hear the car horns and people yelling "Get off the fucking road." Little compares to the exhilaration of listening to Queen's 'Bicycle' while riding in the centre of a lane at half the speed limit with several hundred cars banked up behind me during peak hour traffic. Riding a bicycle is also an excellent way to quickly go downhill.

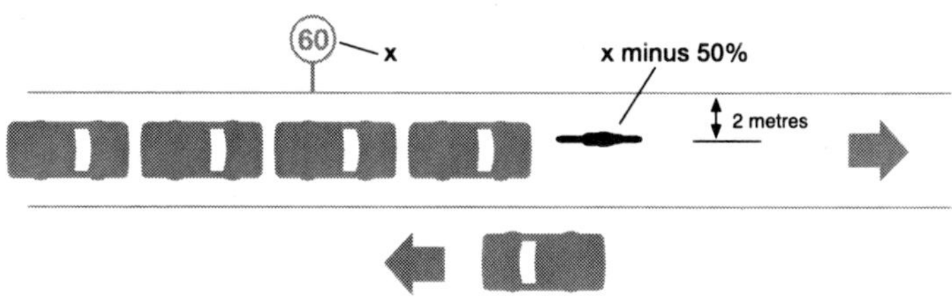

Correct bicycling speed and position

I am often asked why my Spandex® bicycle riding costume features eight hundred and thirty corporate sponsorship logos even though I do not actually have a sponsor. The reason for this is simple. For every thirty male bicycle riders there is one female bicycle rider and, as in nature where the most adorned peacock gets the peahen, the male bicycle rider with the most brightly coloured Spandex® and most corporate sponsorship logos gets to mate with her.

Things that are almost as good as riding my bicycle:
1. Looking at my bicycle
2. Talking about my bicycle
3. Watching television programs that feature people riding bicycles
4. Cheese

Road safety is an important component and basic precaution needs to be undertaken. Once when I was riding my bicycle at great speed, I developed speed wobble and was thrown, rolling several times and sliding several metres, towards a busy intersection. I was lucky enough not to enter the flow of traffic thanks only to friction. As bicycles do not come with safety airbags, I now carry an inflatable raft and pump with me at all times. A lot of people choose not to ride a bicycle because they are too embarrassed to wear a crash helmet but by painting the helmet light brown, it can easily be disguised as a large mushroom.

People often say to me "That's a nice bicycle John" and I reply, "Yes, it is made out of a titanium composite alloy such as NASA uses on the space shuttle and it has Shimano gears which are the best." Just a few weeks ago, while I was taking a rest from riding my bicycle on a park bench, a man walking past said to me "That's a nice bicycle, can I take it for a ride? I will bring it right back" and I said "Sure, but be careful because it is made out of a titanium composite alloy such as NASA uses on the space shuttle and it has Shimano gears which are the best."

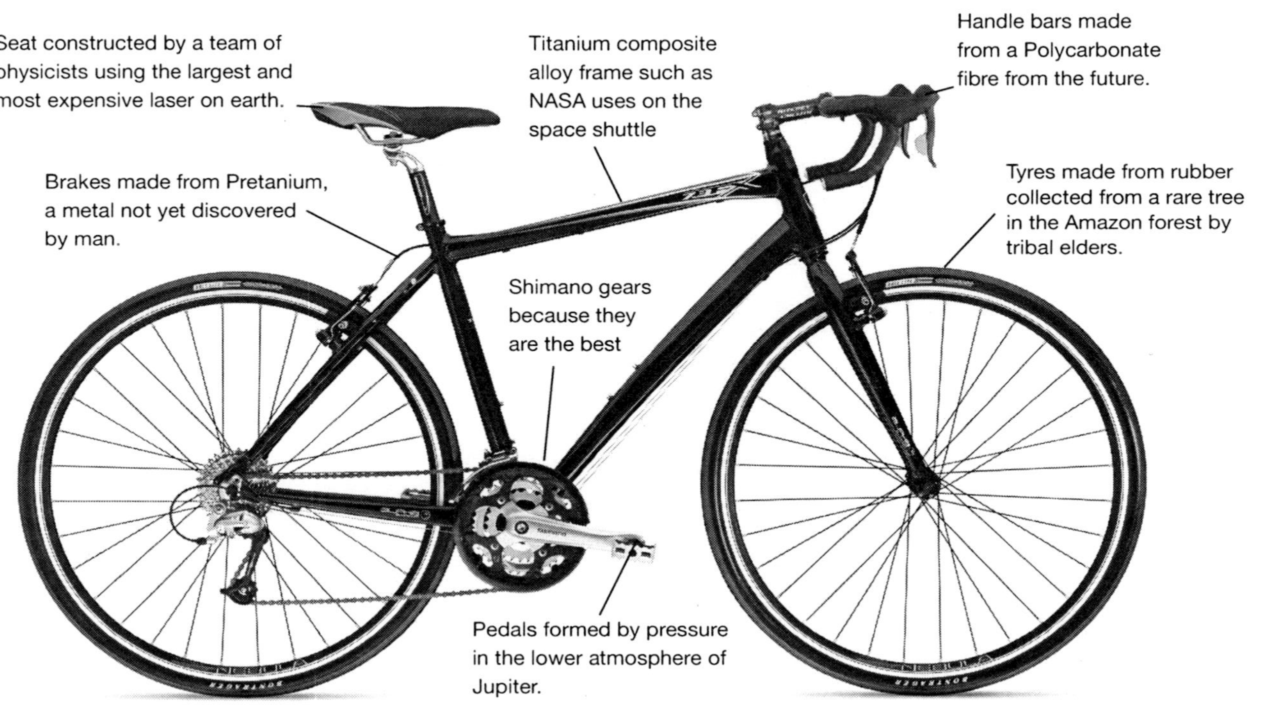
Seat constructed by a team of physicists using the largest and most expensive laser on earth.
Titanium composite alloy frame such as NASA uses on the space shuttle
Handle bars made from a Polycarbonate fibre from the future.
Brakes made from Pretanium, a metal not yet discovered by man.
Tyres made from rubber collected from a rare tree in the Amazon forest by tribal elders.
Shimano gears because they are the best
Pedals formed by pressure in the lower atmosphere of Jupiter.

Agatha Christie taking a break in between novel 619,287 and novel 619,288

TEN JOBS THAT I WOULD RATHER HAVE THAN MINE

I get up after hitting the snooze button a minimum of six times. I make a coffee, then sit in the shower drinking it and smoking cigarettes until the initial agony of knowing I have to spend another day with my coworkers dissipates. I generally spend this time trying to calculate the pros and cons of just not turning up. I know they will bitch but their opinions mean little to anyone so sometimes I just stay in the shower for an hour and then go back to bed. If I do decide to go in, I sit in an office the size of a wardrobe and temperature of a kiln prostituting myself by spending the day making poor products look appealing so that people will be tricked into buying them. This pretty much sums up the entire design industry. Sometimes I grumble and whine out loud so that people think I am working but I will be on the internet instead. It has lots of things on there I like. As I am possibly the laziest person I know, the design industry is only field I can survive in. I would last less than an hour doing manual labour of any form and I often cope on less than two hours sleep a night so anything requiring alertness or intelligence is out of the question. As is anything requiring personal hygiene. This leaves either taxi driver or my boss's position. As his job role consists only of pretending to talk on the phone, passing blame and downloading pornography, I am more than qualified.

#1 Fortune Cookie Writer

As far as writing jobs go, this would probably be the easiest as the pages are very small. When I was at school, I had an English teacher named Judith Bowman who would make us read a novel every few weeks and write a two page essay on each. This would not usually be an issue, as I enjoy reading, but Mrs Bowman loved Agatha Christie novels so would force us to read only these. As my interest in reading about French inspectors on trains is on equal par with being molested by a drunk uncle, I handed in my two page essay on two pieces of paper measuring two by three centimetres each (arguing that the size of the two pages had not been indicated at any time) with the words "Reading the novel Murder on the Orient Express was" on one piece, and "less enjoyable than being molested by a drunk uncle." on the other. This did not go down as well as might have been expected and I was forced to re-write the essay which this time I began with "Being forced to read Mrs Bowman's own personal preferences in literature is less enjoyable than being molested by a drunk uncle which is why I chose to read Enders Game by Orson Scott Card instead..." If I was a professional fortune cookie writer, amongst the standard messages of promised hope and riches, I would include statements such as "I am sending you this message from the future, robots will take over in four days, leave the city immediately." and "Judith Bowman has anal warts".

#2 Park Ranger

Sometimes when I am at work and I have had enough of moving pixels around the screen, I will grab my keys and say "I have to go to a client meeting, I will be back in an hour" and run out the door before anybody can question who the meeting is with. Then I go shopping for cleaning products or to a movie. If I was a park ranger I would tell everyone that I had a meeting with a sick bear or something then go for a canoe ride or trap squirrels.

#3 Drug Dealer

It would seem to me that being paid to provide something that makes people happy would be one of the most satisfying professions available. A while back, my mother visited a Tasmanian region where they grow opium poppies for medicinal puposes and brought me back me a seed she had 'found'. I planted it in my front yard and several weeks later it bloomed. Having read L.Ron Hubbard's Mission Earth series which included detailed instructions on processing opium, I used a scalpel to cut lines in the black centre then dried the milky substance resulting in about half a teaspoon of white powder. That night, my friend Kas came over to my place with his entire CD collection to listen to and we decided to try some of the powder. A short time later, with the live version of Gary Numan's Down in the Park playing on loop, we were both standing completely naked in the bathroom shaving our entire bodies following a discussion about how nice it would be to have smooth skin like an eel. I do not recall much of the rest of the evening but I awoke to find myself wearing a pillow case with holes cut out for my arms as a shirt and Kas asleep on the sofa wearing the same plus 3D glasses. Before waking and leaving later that afternoon, Kas swapped me his entire CD collection for the remainder of the powder.

#4 Wind Turbine Technician (specialising in aerotechatrons)

Everyone loves wind turbines because they are so big and white and symbolise clean, renewable energy and environmental responsibility. I knew a girl once who had a poster of one on her wall and when I asked if she was an evironmentalist she answered "no, I just like them" which is fair enough. Everyone does. I have never heard anyone say "God I hate wind turbines" so if my business card said Wind Turbine Technician rather than designer, I would probably receive the pity look a lot less. The only problem is that I would have to pretend to care about the environment. There is an old saying that "this is not our planet, we are just looking after it for our children" but in thirty years when my offspring complains that we trashed the planet, I will say "That's what you get for all the crap Fathers day presents."

#5 New Zealand Tourism Operator

This would give me plenty of spare time as nobody wants to go there.

#6 Adult Movie Star

Being paid to do something pleasurable would be nice so it is strange that prostitution or starring in pornographic movies is seen as a demeaning profession. While attending uni, studying the artistic equivelent of prostitution (graphic design), a female friend and I decided to make a 'home video' and borrowed a large video camera with tripod from the university media department for the night. Foregoing script, we were in mid performance when my leg developed a severe cramp and I kicked the tripod causing the camera to topple forward and crash into the back of my head head cutting a two inch gash. I was kept at the hospital overnight after receiving fourteen stitches and arrived home the next day to find the camera had been returned to the media department complete with video cassette still in it. A week later, I received a letter from the media department lecturer stating that that the media equipment is available only for school projects and not "C grade pornography".

#7 Parking Inspector

Although there would obviously be many benefits to being a parking inspector, the knowledge that every day I would be making the world a better place would be the most satisfying aspect. They would try to pay me and I would put my hand up and say "No, the important contribution I make to society is payment enough."

#8 Accident Claim Investigator

Having a job where people tell you a story and you say "I don't think so" seems like it would be a lot of fun. I have been in a total of three vehicle accidents. The first occured when I was driving on a dirt road in the rain, lost control and hit a cow. The second involved forgetting to set the handbrake and a river. The third and most recent accident occured while driving home from my friend Simon's place. While at his house for a coffee, I attached a black rubber spider on string to the inside of his cupboard with sticky tape so that the next time he opened it to grab a coffee mug, the spider swung out at him. The reaction was more than expected as Simon screamed, threw himself backwards onto the floor and actually sobbed a little. Later that afternoon as I was driving home, I lowered the sun visor and the rubber spider, which Simon had placed there in what he felt was appropriate retaliation, fell forward onto my lap. My immediate reaction was to press hard on the brake and turn the steering wheel which sent the vehicle into a spin before clipping a white Mercedes and ending up in an elderly man's front hedge. On all three occasions I have been assigned an accident claim investigator.

#9 Forest Fire Lookout

As far as I can tell, the position consists entirely of sitting in a very tall cubby house looking out the window. As you would be able to see for miles around and tell if anyone was coming, you could do anything you wanted in between reporting over the radio that you have not seen any forest fires yet. I would probably watch a lot of pornography and do drugs. When I was about ten, a friend of mine and I built a cubby house in the tallest tree in our backyard using wooden planks stolen from the neighbours fence. Late one evening, while my parents were at a marriage councelling session, I was in the cubby house (as it overlooked the neighbour's bedroom) when a strong breeze caused the cubby house to collapse and pin me between the floor and a fallen wall. Unable to call out or move due to the crushing weight, I remained there the entire night, falling asleep at one point but waking when it started to rain, before finally being rescued the next day when the neighbour let his cat out and heard my soft cries for help. While I was at the hospital being checked over, the neighbour took back his planks.

#10 Doctor

Because nurses are easy.

RUMOUR THAT THOMAS TAKES A PHOTO OF CAROL BRADY TO THE HAIRDRESSER PROVEN UNFOUNDED

Here is finally conclusive evidence that there are indeed considerable differences between the two haircuts. Tom's hair is a shade darker and Carol's has slightly more body - possibly due to the two using different shampoo and conditioning products - Carol uses Johnson & Johnson brand while Thomas uses the natural oils from his body which Lillian harvests for him using a custom made spatula.

Note:
This page does not take into account the dimensional differences between Carol and Tom's heads.

Photographic Evidence 1
Shows Tom's hair does not have highlights towards the sides.
Photographic Evidence 2
shows Carol Brady's hair has a lighter hue with highlights towards the sides.

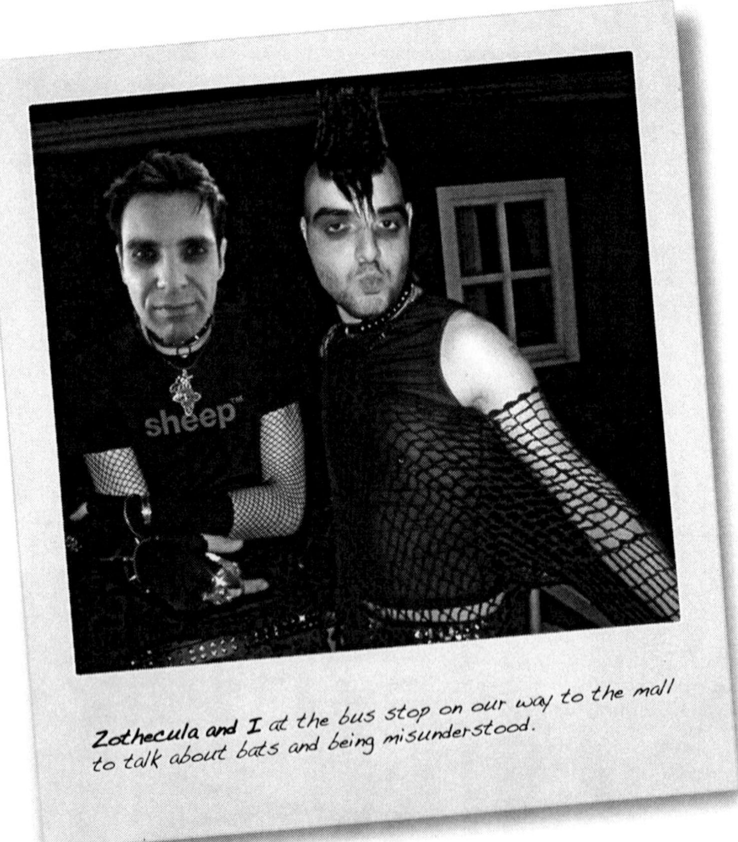

Zothecula and I at the bus stop on our way to the mall to talk about bats and being misunderstood.

KALETH THE ADELAIDE GOTHIC

Hello, my name is Kaleth. My real name is Darryl but my friends call me Kaleth. I asked them to and some of them said they would. I am a vampire and a creature of the night which is why my friend Zothecula and I stand in the middle of the mall during the day discussing bats and being misunderstood.

My cousin Justin wants to be a gothic as well but you can't just become a gothic, you are either creative and sensitive like I am or you are not. I agreed to meet him at the mall to stand in the middle and discuss bats and being misunderstood but when he got there it was obvious that his top was actually very dark blue and not black so I did not let him.

Yesterday, while we were standing in the middle of the mall discussing bats and being misunderstood, a group of people called me an Emu. I looked it up on google and it turns out that it is a bird that can't fly so they were wrong because I can fly. Once, when I was a bat, I flew to my friend Zothecula's house and tapped on his window. The next day he told me that he saw a bat outside his window and I told him that it was me but he didn't believe me.

Zothecula and I are going to live forever because we are both vampires. We met on an internet chat site called batsandbeingmisunderstood.com last year and now we regularly catch the bus to the mall to stand in the middle and discuss bats and being misunderstood together. I met my internet girlfriend Nightblade on the same site and we had planned to get married in a graveyard at midnight but she turned out to be an old guy living in a caravan so that didn't work out.

I was playing my Best of Siouxsie and the Banshees cassette really loud the other day while doing some gothic dancing and my neighbour slipped a note under my door that read "turn it down Batman". He calls me Batman because I painted my front door black with bats on it so that it looks like they are flying out of a cave. One of the bats has my face on it and my best friend Zothecula said that it is the best painting he has ever seen. If my neighbour knew that I could cast a magic spell that would just kill him straight away, he would be more careful.

Yes, us gothics are more intelligent and sensitive than you and we do look at things differently, but that doesn't mean that we can't all get along. We understand you so I think you should at least try to understand us.

On the next few pages are some of my paintings. I do them to show others the pain and torment I experience.

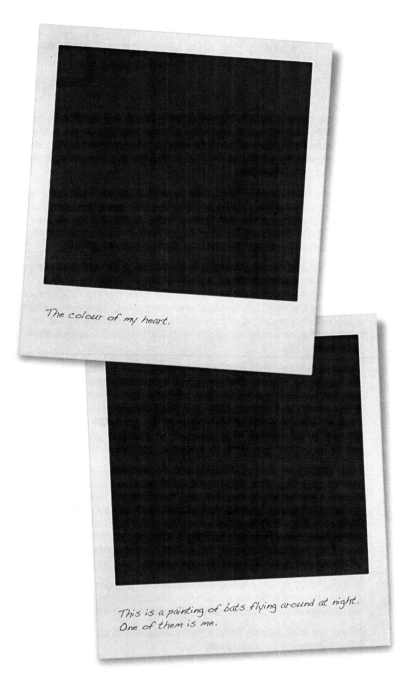
The colour of my heart.
This is a painting of bats flying around at night.
One of them is me.

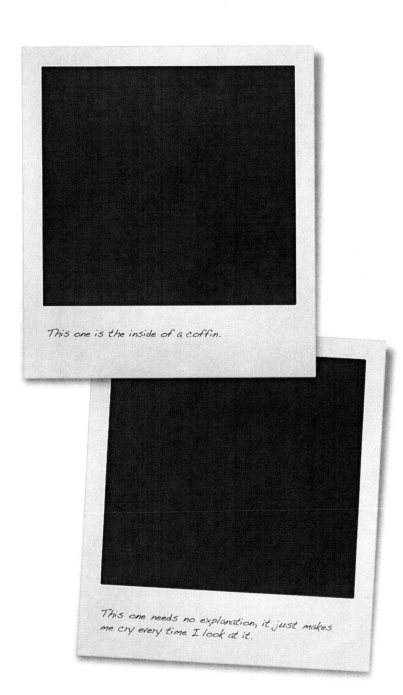
This one is the inside of a coffin.
This one needs no explanation, it just makes me cry every time I look at it.

Barry Chicken magnet

HAVE YOU EVER NOTICED HOW BEAUTIFUL A BABY'S SMILE IS?

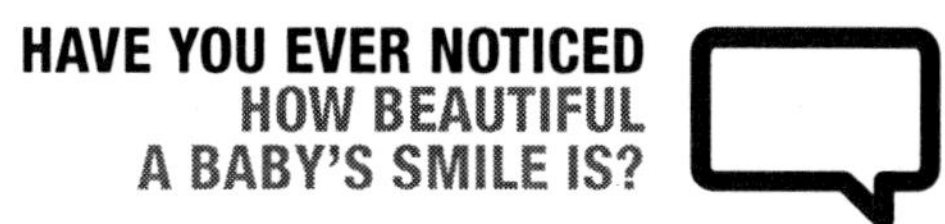

Hello, my name is Barry, I am available and looking for that special woman. She has to enjoy never leaving the house, cleaning me with a damp cloth and experiencing the beauty of a baby's smile. I placed an ad in the singles columns that simply read 'Woman wanted'. I felt it would be superficial to include that she must be athletic and named Candy, I will screen them when they call.

I read recently that the earth is not actually a sphere and is compressed at the poles and bulges at the equator where the world spins the fastest. This means that objects at the equator are under less gravitational pull and therefore weigh less. I have calculated that I would lose almost six hundred kilos by moving my bed ten metres closer to the equatorial line. This is a lot of effort for little outcome but I did change position by eight centimetres today. Changing positions once a week allows mum to wipe sections of my body according to a rotation schedule. It also burns calories and is part of my regular exercise routine.

In the future, there will be televisions that change channels when you blink your eyes.

My Life Story

I was born in a small village near a secret government testing complex. As part of an experiment in human/pig cloning, I led a happy childhood, often seen rolling through the streets of the village. Sometimes I would also take my scooter. When I grew to manhood, I was placed inside a magnetically shielded device designed to compress my molecular structure into a singularity point using my body's own gravitational fields.

Now that I am a singularity point, I have the ability to see through all time and space.

The View From My Bed *A Poem by Barry*

I have two buckets, green and blue.
On Tuesdays a nurse comes and cleans my poo.

My Favourite Bible story

Once when baby jesus was in the desert, he turned some snakes into a small hut where he lodged for the night.

Bill's guide to the internet

Hello, my name is Bill and welcome to my guide to the internet. Basically, everything on the internet is rubbish but I will try to pinpoint the main areas to avoid. The internet is full of idiots writing rubbish for other idiots to read. If I want to find something out I will ask someone or read a book. I paid over three thousand dollars for my complete leather bound set of Funk & Wagnalls in 1967 and if it is not in there then it is not worth knowing. Also, man will walk on the moon before I have a facebook page.

Google

When I was young and I wanted to know something, I was beaten for being too inquisitive. That's the problem with the young people today, they have a google answer for everything. If they had to walk to their local library every time they had something stupid to ask they would ask a lot less stupid questions.

Google Images

Google Images is useless. I used it once to search for a photo of farm equipment and it showed me twenty thousand pictures of horse dicks.

Blogging

I read a blog once by someone who had bought a scarf and he went on for about three hundred paragraphs about his scarf and where he bought it and how it made him feel. The last time I bought a scarf I wore it. End of story. I didn't write a novel about it.

Chatrooms

If I wanted to chat with strangers, I would pick up the phone and press random numbers. I tried a chatroom once and was talking to guy who claimed he was an obese fifty three year old man living in a caravan park but there is no way of knowing if these people are telling the truth.

The Bath Mat

I realise this is not internet related but I cannot understand why it is so hard for people to hang the bath mat over the bath when they are finished using it. I don't leave the mat all soggy for other people to walk on after I have been in there.

Twitter
Why would I want anybody I don't know knowing what I am doing? I don't yell out to everyone in the supermarket "I am buying oranges" so why would I want to do it on my internet? When I was young, I lived in a small village where everybody knew each other and knew what everyone was up to. There was a fat italian kid who lived next door to me named Tony. One day I shot him in the leg with a home made bow & arrow from my treehouse that overlooked his yard and his parents called the police. Within hours the entire village was calling me William Tell. Having escaped the small town mentality for the last fifty two years, I am hardly going to advertise my movements now.

Facebook
I have a photo album on my bookshelf full of faces of people I know which I haven't opened since 1982 so why would I want their faces on my internet? None of them are even very good looking. I tried facebook to see what all the fuss was about and was only on there five minutes before some idiot poked me. It is easy to be brave when you are on the internet.

Reddit / Digg
These sites are the online equivalent of walking down the street, finding a rock shaped like a frog and holding it up in the air while yelling for all my neighbours to come out and tell me what they think of my frog shaped rock. My neighbours can all go to hell. Especially Mrs Carter in number three who leaves her bins out all week. If I did find a rock shaped like a frog, I would throw it at her.

eBay
If I wanted a house full of cheap, dirty, second hand rubbish,
I would go to a garage sale in Klemzig.

Email
People are always sending me all kinds of rubbish. Why would I want dozens of pictures of lots of love cats? I hate cats. I went away for a week recently and when I got back and checked my email, I had eight hundred and forty three messages. Eight hundred and forty of these were adverts for viagra and the other three were pictures of lots of love cats. I bought a 'no junk mail' sticker and stuck it on my modem but nobody has taken any notice.

/b/
I spent a good hour on this site and still have no idea what it is for. All I could work out is that I am apparently a newfag and cannot triforce but am unsure as to why I would need to triforce in the first place.

THOMAS THE PSYCHIC KARATE SOLDIER WHO CAN FLY
BY THOMAS

TOM'S DIARY
A WEEK IN THE LIFE OF A BUSY CREATIVE DIRECTOR

Hello, my name is Thomas and I run a design agency. You have probably heard of me as I am known as the Design Guru of Adelaide. Everybody calls me that. You can call me Tommy though. Or the Design Guru of Adelaide if you want. Just try it and see how it sounds. No? Ok, I wasn't asking you to call me that, I was just saying most people do. It's not a problem, Tommy then. Or the Design Guru of Adelaide if you say it a few times in your head and find you prefer it because it rolls off the tongue quite well. Ok, Tommy then. Yes, Thomas is fine.

Jan 18 Monday

10.30am
At work early this morning as I started writing a novel last night and am keen to check if any publishers have emailed me with expressions of interest yet. I am about half way through and so far it is brilliant. It is about a guy who runs a design agency during the day but at night is a karate soldier with psychic powers. And can fly. And has lots of girlfriends. I am currently searching through photos of me for an appropriate one to use on the cover. One that says 'creative genius' but at the same time 'hey'. I will probably use the one where I am sitting on a chair as it will remind people of that statue where the guy is thinking called Guy Thinking. Or the one of me on the beach as my hair looks great and I am not wearing a shirt which will sell books.

12.30pm
Have just ordered a new MacBook Pro as my current one is almost six months old and I cannot be expected to play Solitaire at these speeds. Staff complained about the speed of theirs when they heard but I spend four to five hours each day sitting behind them watching what they do and have witnessed first hand Photoshop running fine on the Macintosh IIci they share. I just upgraded it to 8Mb a few years ago and am far too busy to be dealing with their petty issues.

1.30pm
Spent the last hour furiously writing another chapter of my novel. It now spans several millenia, from the nineteeth century to the twentieth, due to the main character being immortal. Having him first jousting redcoats then, later in the novel, time travelling robots, provides contrast and a break from the parts where he has a lot of girlfriends.

2.30pm
Have been sitting behind the staff having brilliant ideas. I think of things all the time that are brilliant. What is it called when you are a sideways thinker? I am one of those. I usually have about ten sideways ideas per minute. I should probably sit the exam for Mensa. I am just too busy. Just this morning, while shaving my back, I thought how great it would be if my shaver had an mp3 player built in as I was in the mood for a bit of Seal and that would have made the four and a half hour process more enjoyable. I would call it the Rave'n'Shave.

3.30pm
Heading out for a drive shortly to buy a kite as they are a great way of meeting new friends. I have a meeting scheduled but have told the secretary that if the client comes in before I get back, to make small talk about me and say "I am surprised you managed to get an appointment with him as he is in high demand and is known as the Design Guru of Adelaide."

4.30pm
Got back in time for client meeting, we agreed on a package that saves me 20% on local calls so it has been a successful day. Heading home as I am exhausted and Jumper is on cable.

Jan 19 Tuesday

12.30pm
Just got into the office as I was up late downloading the iPhone developers kit. I played a lot of Space Invaders on my Commodore 64 when I was young and have a brilliant idea for an app that will make millions of dollars. It is a bit like Space Invaders but more like Frogger. With a Braille touch screen for the blind.

1.30pm
Spent an hour writing another chapter of my novel. The main character now works as an international fashion model. And has the ability to transport himself to any location on the planet as long as he has been there before.

2.30pm
As my creative energies are too large to be tethered to one discipline, in addition to becoming a famous author, I have decided to win Australian Idol this year. I have my first singing lesson in half an hour. My voice is like one of those mermaids that sings to sailors as they crash onto rocks. But a man version with deeper voice and legs. Although I have the look they are after and perfect pitch and tenor, it makes sense to get a few pointers from a professional beforehand.

3.30pm
Have decided not to win Australian Idol this year as I am too busy.

4.00pm
Long day. Heading home after I send out an email to all staff reminding them to refer to me as the Design Guru of Adelaide and describe working with me as inspiring when they talking about me with people at the pub or during family dinners.

Jan 20 Wednesday

11.00am
Late one last night. Decided to go to the pub and stayed for a few drinks even though everyone I knew was leaving when I got there. Guys are uneasy being around me with their girlfriend because they know their girlfriend is thinking about me naked. Probably lifting weights or dancing. Luckily, there was a girl at the bar by herself so I sat down and talked to her about me. Surprisingly, she had not heard of me even though I am very well known and people refer to me as the Design Guru of Adelaide. Unfortunately, she had to leave before she could finish reading the news clippings about me that I keep in my pocket but she did agree to give me her mobile number, 0123 456789, so will ring her tonight and talk about me then.

1.40pm
Staff member just mentioned that eight years ago I said "I have full body cancer with only one year to live and that's why everybody needs to work quicker." Told them that I never said that and to stop making things up. Anyway, I was talking about another guy who had cancer. He is dead now so they should show some respect.

2.00pm
Leaving early today to ring the girl I met last night. She will probably want to meet for a drink or come over to my place so I need to collate the photocopies of news clippings and magazine articles about me into a scrapbook for her and shampoo my chest. I also need to make a mix tape of my favourite songs. I know most of the dance moves to *Disco* by the Pet Shop Boys so will start slow with that before popping and locking for her with some Depeche Mode.

Jan 21 Thursday

9.30am
Early night last night. Walked into the office talking on phone, telling client I appreciate him for saying I was the most creative and brilliant person in Australia, when the phone rang. Explained to staff that my phone is one of the new iPhones that rings while you are on a call to let you know that someone else is calling and they just haven't heard of it yet. Because their phones are old. And I got cut off at the same time it rang. That's the only reason I stopped talking and looked suprised.

10.30am
Finishing up the final chapters of my novel. It is now set in a post-apocalyptic future where the polar ice caps have melted, water covers the planet and people live in floating towns.

11.00am
I have a meeting to go to in an hour and need to go shopping for something nice to wear as my green trucker hat does not go with any of my canvas shoes. I should start my own t-shirt company because I have lots of brilliant ideas for t-shirt designs and people would be happy to pay upwards of two hundred dollars per shirt if they knew I had designed it. Like Ed Hardy. Except I would have cats on mine as cats are very popular. I would sell them online and everytime someone googled my name it would come up with my t-shirt company and they would buy them. I should also make a website where people can buy my semen. Women would pay thousands for my semen. Because of my creative genes. Like one of those race horses or a cow with award winning udders. I would do that if I wasn't so busy.

4.30pm
Have just gotten back from a four hour meeting with a potential client in regards to designing a business card for them. I am very excited about where this could lead as they are the eighteenth largest supplier of gravel in both the east and east-west suburbs of Adelaide. I will send them a quote in a few weeks as they take a long time to write. I could tell they were impressed during the meeting, especially when I explained the need to incorporate cats into the design, as they continually rose, in a manner that can only be described as lengthy standing ovations, then sat down again when I kept talking. One of the female clients was very attracted to me so I spent an hour showing her colour photocopies of my Smart Roadster specs and explained what all the graphs meant. I will send her an email now and tell her my last girfriend died of cancer or something so that she knows I am available and will attach a photo of me sitting in my car. And one of me wearing jogging shorts so she knows I am athletic.

4.35pm
Heading home as I am exhausted both physically and mentally after two client meetings in as many months.

Jan 22 Friday

10.30am
Walked in and had an argument with the secretary. I do not see why I have to justify myself to her. It is my business and therefore my company Visa card. I do not appreciate being questioned. Obviously there has been some kind of mistake and we have been charged $29.95 per month by teenshemale.com in error. It is not her job to ring the bank and question the purchase when I told her I would take care of it even though I am extremely busy.

10.35am
Have put a password on my computer. Used a random selection of 128 numbers and characters so as to make it impossible for the secretary to guess. Will not write it down anywhere in case she finds it.

1.30pm
Completed my novel. It is without a doubt the best book ever written and will become a best seller within weeks. This will mean that I will be very busy doing promotional tours and replying to people who have written thanking me for sharing my gift so I will need to tell my staff that I will not be here as often to give them the creative guidance they rely on me for. This will be upsetting but they have to understand that I owe it to my fans to do book signing tours and appear on *Dancing with the Stars*.

1.35pm
To celebrate the completion of my novel, I invited the staff over to my place to listen to stories about me but they all had prior plans.

2.00pm
Heading home and calling it a week. It has been a very busy one and therefore productive. Next week is going to be extremely busy as I have decided to write a musical based on my life story. Probably with cats in it as cats are very popular.

HIGHLIGHTS OF SOUTH AUSTRALIA
PART 1:
MONARTO ZOO

How is it that Victoria and Queensland can even hope to compete for tourism dollars when South Australia is home to THE Montarto Zoo? Featuring a theoretical plethora of wild beasts, sitting on an ex schoolbus with fifty other people as you drive through gates is exactly like being on an actual savana in South Africa.

Monarto Zoo is always coming up with new advertising to get people to visit. The problem is that when people do visit, they come back and tell people that there are no animals there. If I was the manager of Monarto Zoo, I would have photographic, lifesize cardboard cutouts of animals placed throughout the park and drive the bus too fast for people to notice they are not real. Once word got out that Monarto 'does actually have animals' and people started visiting, we could afford to replace the cardboard animals with animatronic animals.

My son and I went to Monarto Zoo thinking we could drive around the park in our car like you see people in the movies do, having a monkey try to pull off one of our side mirrors or lions lying on our bonnet.

You board a thirty year old schoolbus bus then wait forty minutes for it to fill with people. We were especially lucky to be sitting opposite a mum with a baby that had bright yellow feces leaking out from its diaper.

The bus travels for about ten minutes before stopping to open gates. This happened about twenty times before we saw what was possibly a giraffe lying down. It was too far away to tell whether it was alive and a few children started asking if it was ok so the bus drove on.

The gate system is worth mentioning as it consists of driving up to a gate and pressing a button, the gate rolls open over the space of several minutes and the bus drives through to the next gate and waits for the previous gate to close before opening the gate in front. As this happens at least seventy times, it should be added as a key highlight in promotional brochures.

After another several gates we saw a shed that apparently had a rhino in it which was quite exciting. We then entered several gates and saw some goats. After an hour and several more gates, we returned to the centre where we could buy stuffed animals made in china.

When his grandma asked him what the best part had been, my son replied "The drive home" which I thought was pretty funny but he wasn't joking.

Black Panther
Or possibly a shadow.
An African White Rhinocerous
Or possibly a cow.
Mother and litter of Cheetah babies
Or complete bullshit.

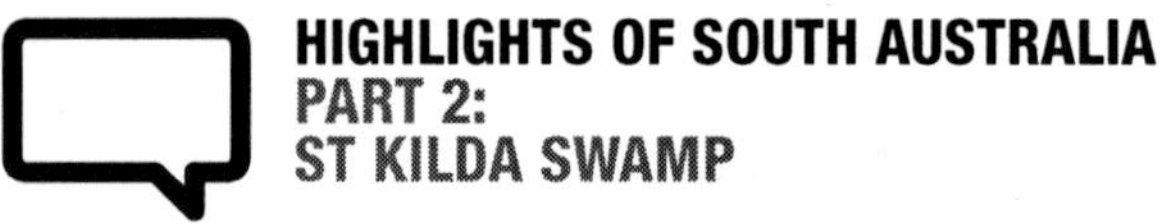

HIGHLIGHTS OF SOUTH AUSTRALIA PART 2: ST KILDA SWAMP

Only forty minutes drive from the city is one of Adelaides most enticing tourist attractions. For a reasonable admission fee of around twenty dollars, families can walk through a swamp along a looping boardwalk. Not all the way of course because the boardwalk is broken in places but the high likelihood of the boardwalk collapsing at any moment only adds to the excitement.

On arrival at the St Kilda mangroves, you make your way through the Interpretive Centre where they have mud and insects displayed so that you can see them before you enter the swamp. Unfortunately, the day we went the Interpretive Centre was closed, probably due to the staff having a meeting about mud and insects. A sign informed us that they were sorry about not being there but we could enter the swamp via a side gate after leaving money in an honour tin. Though my son attempted to access the contents, it was firmly padlocked.

Checkpoint 1

Passing several signs warning us of snakes, we reached the boardwalk and entered the swamp. After pretending to push each other off the boardwalk into the mud for several minutes, we reached the first check point. Checkpoints consist of a slightly wider section of the boardwalk with a sign explaining that the swamp contains mud and insects. There are twenty checkpoints.

Checkpoints 2 to 8

The mud is worth mentioning as there were hardly any insects the day we visited. It is very deep in parts and not in others and has millions of spiky roots sticking out of it like semi submerged hedgehogs. According to the brochure, the mud is teeming with life but we did not see any. Interestingly enough, the brochure also mentioned that dolphins enter the swamp in search of food but as they would require one of those ride-on boats with a big fan on the back like the dad drove in the television series Gentle Ben, this is quite unlikely. The people who wrote the brochure covered themselves though, each statement regarding the wide and exciting range of animals to be seen began with "Depending on weather conditions..." so they could have added tigers, polar bears and elk to the list without any risk of litigation. We did see a dead cat but that was not listed in the brochure.

Checkpoint 9

Despite the noticeable lack of other visitors to the swamp, as we progressed to checkpoint nine, a father and two children approached us along the boardwalk from the opposite direction and we gave each other a sympathetic and understanding nod as we passed.

Checkpoints 10 to 14

While traversing the next few checkpoints, we played a game called 'what we could be doing instead'.

Seb & Holly take a break from their mobile phones and games consoles to pose for a photo in one of the more picturesque regions. The natural beauty reflected in the wonder on their faces.

Checkpoints 15 to 19

We progressed through checkpoints fifteen to nineteen fairly quickly, driven on by the fact that I was experiencing nicotine withdrawal and had left my cigarettes in the car. With only one checkpoint to go, and the car in view, we came to a dead end where the boardwalk had collapsed. Despite seriously considering jumping the five metre gap, braving the millions of spiky roots sticking out of the mud, we were forced to turn back and retrace our journey.

Checkpoints 19 to 1

On the way back we pretended to push each other off the boardwalk into the mud and as Seb was annoying me, I pushed him off the boardwalk into the mud. Due to his new sneakers being cased in twelve inches of solid black mud, he did not speak to me for the rest of the walk back which was nice.

Professor Thomas Master of Science

PROFESSOR THOMAS
EXPLAINS THE MYSTERIES
OF SCIENCE

Hello, my name is Professor Thomas. People ask me many scientific questions and I know all the answers because I have the Discovery Channel at home. Perhaps you would like to come over and watch it with me. I have a rooftop as well.

Perpetual Motion
"Is perpetual motion like when you fall down a bottomless pit?"

"Kind of, but it's more like when you put two ice cubes next to each other, and they'll never melt because they'll just keep each other cold forever."

"What if you put two ice cubes next to each other and dropped them down a bottomless pit?"

"They would drift apart and melt, unless you glued them, but then they wouldn't really be touching."

Leap Years
"I like having an extra day, why can't we have them every year?"

"There is a good reason you only have them once every four years. It's like chocolate. If you have it too often you get too used to it, then you need to eat more. Then we've got too many years and everyone lives too long. This would have serious consequences on the circle of life."

Stars
"There are stars born everyday, people who believe in the science of stars are called scientologists."

Tides
"Sometimes the ocean water is high, but sometimes it's low because the moon is magnetic and it attracts the water."

"I thought magnets only attracted metal."

"Water's a type of metal. It is also one of the noble gases."

The Water Cycle
"Water dies then decomposers break it down into organic matter. Then it rains water seeds, and when the water seeds mix up with the decomposed water, lakes grow."

Hydrogen as a Fuel Source
"Can we use alternative fuel to petrol in our cars?"

"Only certain cars."

"Which cars?"

"Hydrogen is 2/3 of water, so cars that are 1/3 water."

"Really?"

"Yes because humans are 80% water so we use hydrogen and not gasoline, and most cars are around 5%, but if the car is 20% or more water then it can run on hydrogen."

"Like boats?"

"Yes, exactly like boats."

Absolute Zero
"Absolute zero is when it can't get any colder.
It could get infinitely colder, but it wouldn't be anymore cold."

Relativity
"Einstein's theory of relativity is very complicated and can be almost impossible to understand but $E=MC^2$ means when you go really fast, time goes slower because you get there earlier."

Black Holes
"Space is like a bathtub, and you fill it with light, and black holes are where the light drains out."

"Where does the light go?"

"It goes back into space as lightvapor, and when it condensates, that's how a sun is formed."

"So then suns are really clouds of light?"

"Yes, and then they rain sunshine."

BEING BRANDED A SHEEP™

I have always wanted a tattoo. The problem is that I have always considered people who get tattoos as sheep. Especially those that go in and order number fourteen off the wall of a dolphin for example.

I decided that if I was going to be a sheep and get a tattoo, there was only one choice of tattoo to be permanently branded with. I am sure I will still find this amusing in twenty years.

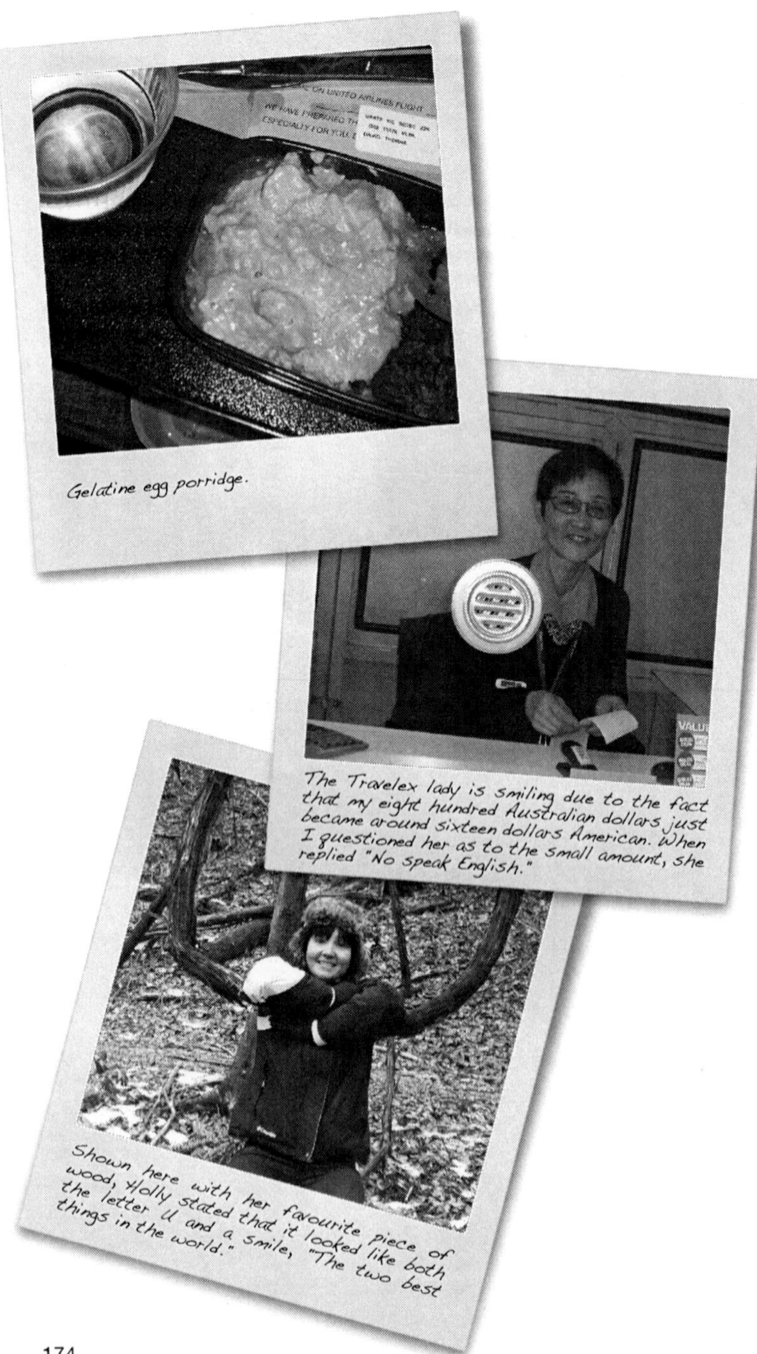

Gelatine egg porridge.

The Travelex lady is smiling due to the fact that my eight hundred Australian dollars just became around sixteen dollars American. When I questioned her as to the small amount, she replied "No speak English."

Shown here with her favourite piece of wood, Holly stated that it looked like both the letter U and a smile, "The two best things in the world."

GUNS, BASEBALL CAPS AND PICKUP TRUCKS
THREE WEEKS IN THE USA

Flying out from Sydney Airport

Sydney Airport incorporates an astonishingly clever luggage trolley system called Smartecarte®. Basically, you pay $4 and load up the trolley then enter the terminal. At this stage you have to go up an escalator that does not fit trolleys. Luckily, after removing your luggage and journeying to the top of the escalator, there is another set of trolleys you can pay $4 to use. You can then use the trolly for a few minutes until you reach the international terminal transfer train that does not allow trolleys onboard. Once the train reaches the international terminal, you pay $4 for a trolley which will enable you to take your luggage around a corner where there is an escalator that does not fit trolleys but has further trolleys at the top for $4 so that you can transport your luggage around two corners before reaching an escalator that does not fit trolleys. Having exhausted both your budget and patience, you carry your bags the rest of the way. Luckily the crowds part for you, due partly to you dripping in sweat, but mainly due to your 'I will stab you' expression, so that you can arrive at the check in counter and pay $230 in excess baggage weight fees.

United Airlines

Many years ago, during a traditional family Christmas gathering, the family dog, named Gus, gained access to and consumed a 1Kg tub of butter that had been left out of the refrigerator. He then proceded to vomit the entire 1Kg up under the table (along with his prior meal of dog food and pieces of Christmas turkey). The similarity, minus a thin piece of three day old tomato and cold spinach, to the gelatine egg porridge I was served on board the fourteen hour United Airlines flight from Sydney to San Francisco was disturbing. I also suspect Gus's version may have contained more nutritional value. Luckily, my meal included a plastic cup of water so using the power of imagination and a plastic spork, I pretended it was a thin soup and made it last for over an hour. Although hungry and bored, I was lucky enough to have an overweight American girl sitting in front of me with her seat reclined thus allowing close inspection of her dandruff. As her hair was very dark, by blurring my eyes I was able to pretend I was looking out of the window at a star filled night and at one point made out the Big Dipper. When she did sit upright for a moment, I opened my laptop with the vague hope that a satellite dish would be pointing at our flying bus allowing me to receive emails but she re-reclined moments later crushing my laptop screen into my wrists so I quietly used gelatine egg porridge to represent the sun on her star map.

Waffle House

Famished after spending a total of thirty six hours on flying buses and waiting in flying bus stations, salvation presented itself in the form of what is, without question, America's finest restaurant chain. If I were a food critic being asked to write about the meal and experience at Waffle House, my review would contain just two words, one being an expletive and the other 'yes'. Possibly accompanied by a pencil sketch of two fat people giving each other a high five. The only negative aspect of the meal was that our waitress, Shauna, hung around and kept going on about her dying child and the cost of cancer medicine in the hope of a large tip but seeing through this ploy, we snuck out without paying and stole a Waffle House coffee mug in the process.

Snow

I had never seen snow before visiting the US and while those around me complained about their vehicles sliding off the road and not being able to get out the front door, I secretly hoped the snow fall would reach several feet and trap me there for months. My first snowball throw ever was a head shot and, taking into account the excellent degree of distance and trajectory analysis, I would have thought my girlfriend Holly would be impressed rather than driving off. Faced with the prospect of spending the night outdoors many miles from civilisation, I built a snowman to ward off wolves while I started work on an igloo. After two hours of work resulting in a pile of snow with a hollowed out cave large enough only for my head, I had to hide my relief when Holly came back, proclaiming to her that I would have been fine due to having read the novel My Side of the Mountain and that I was not crying, it was just a bug or dust or something in my eye.

Walmart

The first time I went to Walmart, I showered, shaved, dressed nicely and did my hair to the bemusement of those with me. The second time, I went unwashed, in my pyjamas, at 3am to buy a gun. In Australia, we have a nationwide ban on anything even remotely gun shaped. When I was about ten years old, there was an elderly man living across the road named Mr Anderson, that I (innocently) drove insane through a sequence of events over twelve months which included painting his windows black believing he would wake up and think it was still night time, tying his lawnmower to the back of his car so he drove off with it and putting several packets of raspberry Jello crystals in his fish pond. The day I dipped tennis balls in paint and threw them at his house obviously broke him and he came out screaming and waving a rifle before being arrested. I did not see Mr Anderson after that but I am sure everything turned out fine and that he looks back on those times with fond memories.

Guns
Having purchased a heavy gauge shotgun and armour piercing rounds from Walmart for the equivalent price of a carton of cigarettes in Australia, I befriended a local farm boy named Chuck by making up aboriginal words and telling lies about Australian fauna (it is now a fact in Virginia that Koalas, known as Boogawigs in the native aboriginal language, communicate with each other through song and weave themselves jackets from gum leaves during winter). Chuck drove us in his red pickup to George Washington Forest to drink beer and kill something. Four drink bottles and a cinder block lost their lives that afternoon before a deer walked into the clearing and was shot in the leg. As the humane thing to do is never leave an animal wounded, and having run out of ammunition, we clubbed it to death with the butt of our rifles, which took about an hour, then tied it to the bonnet of the pickup truck and drove home listening to John Denver while yelling 'Whooo' at pedestrians. Chuck wanted to ritualise my first kill by dipping his finger in the blood and wiping it on my face but as he had done a poo in the forest, without access to hand washing facilities, I told him that as a vegetarian this would not be appropriate.

Philadelphia
Made the long journey from Harrisonburg to Philadelphia for the sole purpose of visiting the famous Love Park. My girlfriend and I fought just hours before due to me stating that I would rather go see the Space Shuttle than visit her family but apparently there is no Pissed Off At David Park. We then drove home during a blizzard using a TomTom GPS system stuck on bicycle mode.

The Space Shuttle
Prior to this trip, the only reason I had ever considered visiting the US was because it has the Space Shuttle. Like a priest carrying home their first computer after hearing about child pornography on the internet, I was practically foaming at the mouth in anticipation during the drive to the Smithsonian Air & Space Museum. I have stood in front of masterpieces in art museums that did not raise an inkling of the emotion I felt at seeing the Space Shuttle. It was at that moment I realised the high horse on which I had laughed at Trekkies from had sidled away in shame. On the way out, after spending the rest of our trip allowance at the museum shop buying plastic products made in China, I pulled my pants high up around my waist, gave my lunch money to a bigger boy and considered going over to Windows®.

PROFESSIONAL PHOTOGRAPHY TIPS WITH THOMAS

Hello, my name is Thomas and I am a professional photographer because I bought a digital camera.

Tip 1 How to become a professional photographer
Buy a digital camera.

Tip 2 Tricks of the trade
Have a look on the camera, somewhere, probably on the top or back or somewhere on the front or sides there will be a button or dial marked 'A', this does not stand for 'Automatic' as some amateurs think but 'Awesome'. Leave it on this all the time.

Tip 3 Photography courses
There is no need for even a basic photography course because once you buy a digital camera you will be a professional photographer like me. Not as good as me though.

Tip 4 Lighting
You will need some light otherwise the photos will come out a bit too dark. Usually you can fix them in photoshop but some light to begin with is good.

Tip 5 Subject Matter
Yes, it does. Don't take photos of girls leaving the high school from your car as the fine is $360 and a years probation.

View of city from my rooftop
Sunset from my rooftop
Some people that visited me on my rooftop. Or my toes. I am unsure.

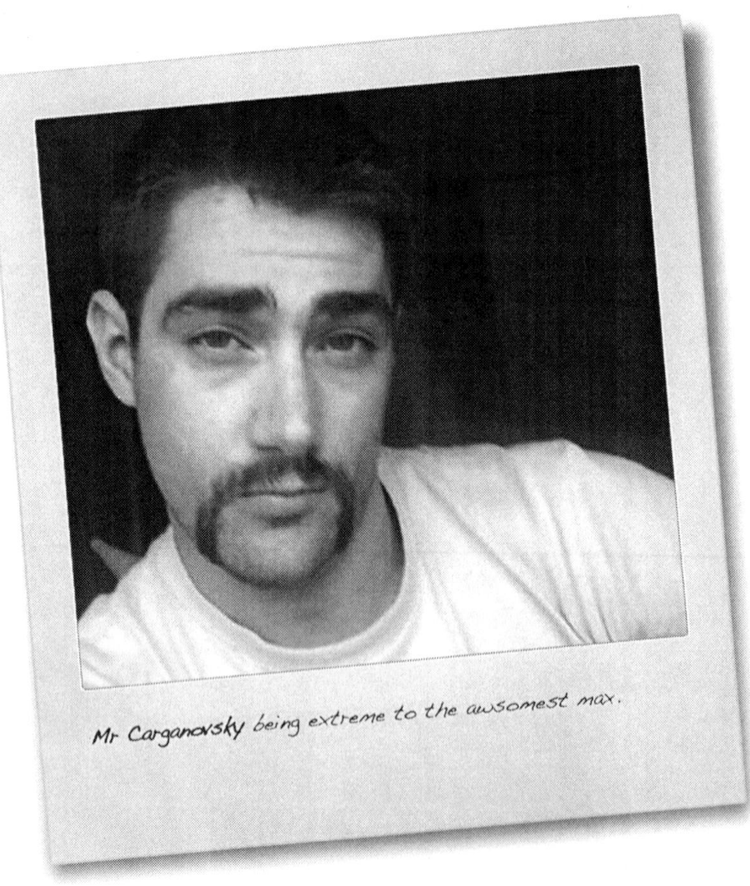

Mr Carganovsky being extreme to the awsomest max.

HELLO, MY NAME IS MR CARGONOVSKY (NOT SKYE CARGAN) AND I AM AUSTRALIA'S MOST EXTREME STUNTMAN TO THE AWESOMEST MAX

If you have a party, wedding or BBQ that you need a show for, please contact me and I will do you a good price. I will soon be famous and the price will go up so be quick. I have been a professional stunt man for nearly four weeks. In that time I have looked death in the face many times. My career began when someone clipped the side mirror of my Datsun 180B while I was parked at a K-Mart. I was inside purchasing credit for my phone at the time and did not notice the cracked mirror until I was driving home. A police car, with sirens and lights flashing, came up behind me before overtaking and due to the refraction caused by the shattered mirror, when I looked I thought there were about forty police vehicles behind me and I almost had an aneurysm. I have a few outstanding parking fines. I swerved and mounted the curb, almost hitting a dog, before bringing the vehicle under control. The dog was on the other side of the road and behind a fence but if it hadn't been, the outcome could have been very different. The adrenalin rush was unlike anything I had ever experienced and I knew I had found my calling. The rest of the way home I drove sixty three even though it was a sixty zone as my yearning for the extreme had been fueled.

My most recent stunts include running on the concrete at my local swimming pool, putting aluminium foil in the microwave, talking to strangers and just last night I lit myself on fire. If you hold a gas lighter in your palm with the button depressed then spark it, the gas ignites for a couple of seconds. My nephews said it was the best trick they have ever seen. To prepare for each stunt, I enter a deep meditative state through circular breathing execises and twelve hours in my friend Simon's floatation tank listening to whale calls. As Simon does not own a tape of whale sounds, he makes the noises himself through a hole in the lid which is quite annoying. I am currently preparing for my latest stunt in which I intend to play with pointy sticks then eat and go swimming without waiting thirty minutes.

Safety is paramount in the stunt business. My car is completely fitted out with a St Johns first aid kit in the glove compartment. The vehicle predates manufacturer requirements for air bags but I have glued several rubber stress balls to my steering wheel and replaced the interior lining with bubble wrap. The car's exterior, engine, transmission and tyres are completely shot but apart from that the vehicle is in excellent condition so it is worth spending money on. Last week I had signwriters paint 'Mr Carganovsky, Exteme Stunt Man to the Awesomest Max' on the side and this has attracted a lot of attention.

I also need to buy a cassette player to play my new theme song while I am doing stunts:

Mr Carganovsky to the Extreme.
By Mr Carganovsky, music by Proclaimers

It's Mr Carganovsky,
Being extreme to the awesomest max,
Did you see what he just he did? No? Pity because it was amazing.
Dont push him, cause he is close to the edge,
Woh!

As I do not currently have a stereo in the car, I am forced to nod my head and tap the steering wheel to disguise the fact at traffic lights so that people do not point and say "Look there's Mr Carganovsky sitting in his car in silence. He must be poor". Also, if I am touching metal when I turn the ignition key, I receive a short but painful shock which often causes me to black out for an hour or two. This accounts for my being late to work at least three times a week and I am on my last warning. I dont care if I get sacked though as I will be famous soon. My job consists of googling pictures of cats for ninety percent of the day and the other ten percent constructing reasons why no work gets done. They have not caught on yet as I hide my browser window by displaying pornography when anybody enters my office. While my co-workers are in production meetings discussing why nothing is produced, I steal office supplies and sell them on eBay using the proceeds to promote my stunt man career. Thanks to a bulk office purchase of liquid paper, I was able to have tshirts made and often I come into work after hours and use the photo copier to print my promotional tour posters. I usually post a few thousand a week on walls and poles around town so the UHU sticks have also come in handy.

With the money I make from being a famous stunt man, I am hoping to one day open a stunt school offering courses such as 'Flicking the Light Switch On and Off Repeatedly' and 'Sitting Too Close to the Television'.

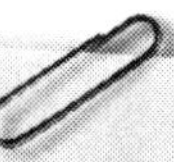

LAWYERS

Mr David Thorne
PO Box 10476 Adelaide BC, South Australia 5000

Reference No. 003972THORNE

23.6.2009

Dear Mr Thorne,
I am writing to you on behalf of our client Skye Cargan. I am under instruction to give you 48 hours in which to remove all references to Mr Cargan from your website 27bslash6.com or we will begin legal proceedings against you. Should you have any questions or response to this request please call during office hours or email me at craig.elli[redacted]m.au

Sincerely,

Craig M. Ellison

From: David Thorne
Date: Friday 26 June 2009 11.02am
To: Craig Ellison
Subject: Skye Cargan

Dear Mr Ellison,

Thankyou for your letter. Does the forty eight hours include sleeping time? I like to sleep in till around midday, often longer if it is cold and rainy outside. Today when I got up it was bitterly cold so I sat on the couch watching Blakes-7 dvds wrapped in my duna and therefore technically still in bed. If I bought two dunas, layed down on them with my arms and legs splayed out, drew the outline of my body then cut out and stitched the dunas together to form a suit, I could wear this to the shops and even to work on cold days. People would probably look at me and say "I wish I had one of those duna suits" and I would say "Yes, it is very warm and comfortable and just like being in bed therefore I am exempt from any deadlines that may be placed on me."

Regards, David.

From: Craig Ellison
Date: Friday 26 June 2009 12.55pm
To: David Thorne
Subject: Re: Skye Cargan

Dear Mr Thorne

The 48 hours includes sleeping time. I would advise you to take this matter seriously as anti harrassment laws are very specific and carry penalites ranging from fines to prison time. You would also be liable for all legal fees.

Sincerely, Craig Ellison

From: David Thorne
Date: Friday 26 June 2009 1.27pm
To: Craig Ellison
Subject: Re: Re: Skye Cargan

Dear Mr Ellison,

Does the forty hours begin from when you wrote the letter, when I received it, or when I chose to ignore it? Despite your inference, I do indeed take your threats very seriously. The thought of spending time in prison has caused my entire body to break out in a rash. It is a brown, even rash which looks like I have been away on holidays and gotten a tan so that is nice. While I am sure prison would have certain benefits, such as not having to decide what to wear each morning and the opportunity to meet new and interesting people, I have heard that they make you get up early and also expect you to shower in front of each other. At home, I shower with the lights off as I have a dim view of nudity. I also read once that the other prisoners make you dress up like a lady and dance for them which does not sound like a safe idea. It has taken me years of practice to just walk in high heels let alone dance. I would probably have to do one of those eighties dances where you just keep your legs still and dance with your arms and upper body and the other prisoners would probably get bored and go and do other things. Unless I did the Robot of course which does not involve moving the feet much and everyone loves the Robot. I only know two other dances; the Matrix where you lean right back waving your arms slowly and the old man dance where I tense up, shuffle my feet intermittently, complain about the music and sit down for a rest. I could probably tap dance as well as it looks easy but nobody likes that rubbish.

Regards, David.

From: Craig Ellison
Date: Friday 26 June 2009 3.06pm
To: David Thorne
Subject: Re: Re: Re: Skye Cargan

Dear Mr Thorne

What does this all have to do with removing our clients name and photo from your website? I would strongly advise you not to ignore our letter. If references to our client are not removed by 5pm Wednesday 7th of July we will file a complaint with the courts pending instruction from Mr Cargan.

Sincerely, Craig Ellison

From: David Thorne
Date: Friday 26 June 2009 4.21pm
To: Craig Ellison
Subject: Re: Re: Re: Re: Skye Cargan

Dear Mr Ellison,

I understand. In the event that this proceeds to court, will you appear for me as a character witness? I enjoy room temperature, pushing buttons with a really smooth push button action and getting a little bit wet in the rain then quickly running inside. Should you require more information, I am happy to meet up with you for a coffee or watch a dvd and discuss further. Have you seen the movie Waterworld? I haven't but I have heard it is terrible so we would not watch that. We could read to each other if you preferred. There is a chance we could even become close friends through this which would be a nice outcome. I read somewhere that lawyers are second only to dentists in regards to committing suicide so you would have someone to talk to when you are down about everyone despising you. I would probably talk you out of committing suicide and you would owe me your life and buy me nice things. I would pretend to feel uncomfortable about accepting them and say "you don't have to feel obligated, that's what friends do" but really I would be quite happy about it. I am a size 32 in pants.

Regards, David.

From: Craig Ellison
Date: Monday 29 June 2009 9.36am
To: David Thorne
Subject: Re: Re: Re: Re: Re: Skye Cargan

David, please just remove the references to Mr Cargan from your website. He has not given you permission to use his image or name. His posting information on Facebook or Myspace does not make that information public property. I have spoken to Mr Cargan in regards to this matter and while it is my understanding that he initiated the contact and the webpage was your response, it would be preferrable to all concerned that you end this now to avoid possible litigation.

Sincerely, Craig Ellison

From: David Thorne
Date: Monday 29 June 2009 10.09am
To: Craig Ellison
Subject: Re: Re: Re: Re: Re: Re: Skye Cargan

Dear Mr Ellison,

I appreciate Mr Cargan's preference for anonymity all to well. Each day before I leave the house, I dress as an elderly Jamaican woman and am well known in the community as Mrs Cocowan. That way, if I ever find myself involved in a major crime, and it is just a matter of time, they will be looking for a large old black lady that sings for money at the train station and can run suprisingly fast. If I change Mr Cargan's identity would this be acceptable to you?

Regards, David.

From: Craig Ellison
Date: Monday 29 June 2009 2.42pm
To: David Thorne
Subject: Re: Re: Re: Re: Re: Re: Re: Skye Cargan

Dear Mr Thorne

I have spoken to Mr Cargan and we agree that changing Mr Cargan's identity would be an acceptable outcome. I am glad we could bring this issue to an agreeable close.

Sincerely, Craig Ellison

BELLY MESSAGES
PRETENDING TO BE AN ATTRACTIVE FEMALE ON THE INTERNET

Internet love can be a beautiful thing but there is no real way of knowing if that attractive young brunette you find yourself smitten with is not actually an eighty-five year old woman with thirty cats. Or a guy.

Username Danni T

Looking For
A guy that prefers to stay at home with me rather than go out. I just want to meet a normal guy that I can be myself around. Looks and age not important. A guy that likes computer games would be good.

Interests
Movies, music, Warcraft, sex, the internet, photography and my pet cat Ross.

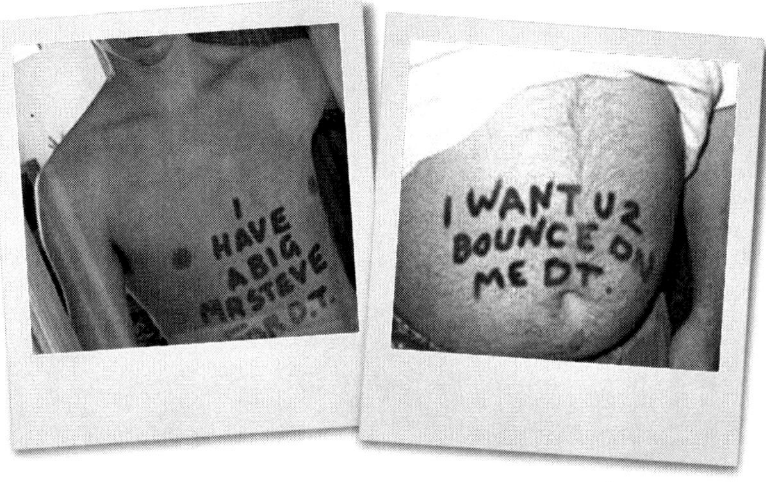

Danni

...I will but first you have to write "I have a big Mr Steve for D.T." on your stomach, take a photo, then email it to me to prove you are genuine.

Hawk410

ok. Whats a Mr Steve? A cock?

Danni

Sigh... yes Jamie.

Hawk410

Do you want my cock in the picture?

Danni

Just your stomach is fine.

Danni

...I would love to bounce up and down on you like a five year old on a jumping castle at a birthday party.

Scott_Mintred

Haha. id fuckn love that to. so are we gonna meet now?

Danni

Definitely but first write "I want you to bounce on me D.T." on your stomach, take a photo, then email it to me to prove you are genuine.

Scott_Mintred

Cool.

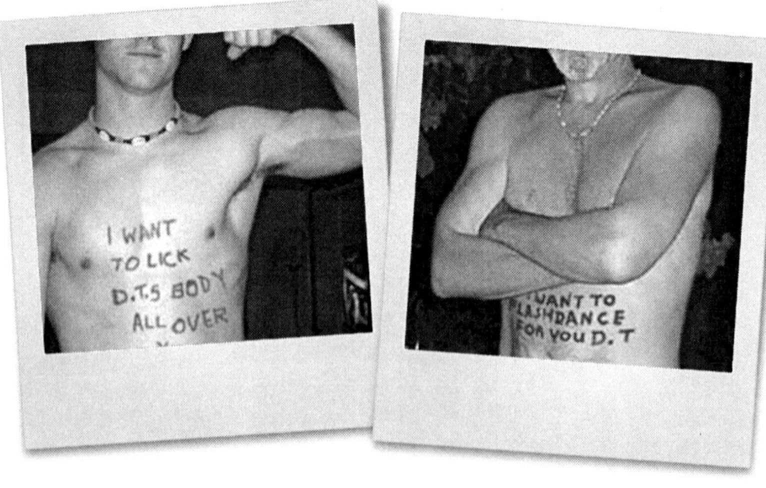

Danni

...as I am very dirty and need somebody to lick my body all over.

Surfkilla

cool! I like dirty girls.

Danni

No, I mean literally dirty, the plumbing is broken and I have not showered in days. First you have to write "I want to lick D.T.'s body all over" on your stomach, take a photo, then email it to me to prove you are genuine.

Surfkilla

ok.

Danni

...yes but first you have to write "I want to flashdance for you D.T." on your stomach, take a photo, then email it to me to prove you are genuine.

Randbgeoff

What the fuck does that mean?

Danni

Um... flashdance means to ejaculate on someones chest I think.

Randbgeoff

Fuck ok. Sorry, I havent heard that one before. Hang on.

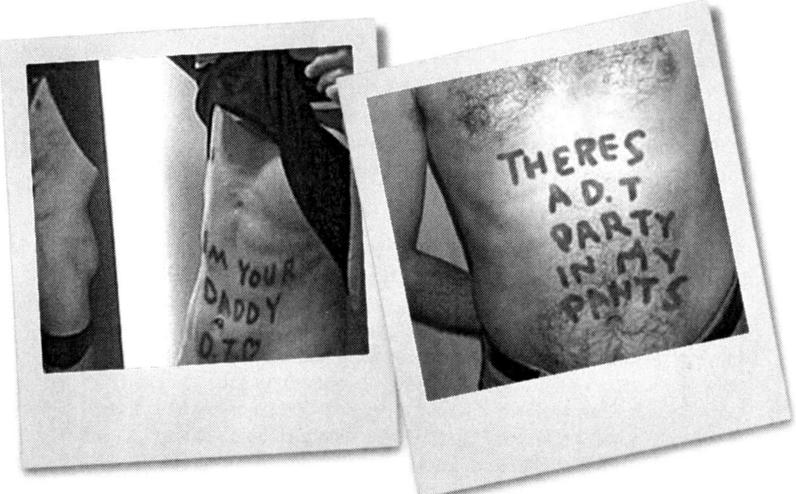

Danni

...will you spank me and tell me that I am a bad girl for spending my money on that Duran Duran record instead of buying you a fathers day present?

Southsidetom

Sure.

Danni

Ok but first write "I am your daddy D.T." on your stomach, take a photo, then email it to me to prove you are genuine.

Southsidetom

No problem babe.

Danni

...yes but first you have to write "There's a D.T. party in my pants" on your stomach, take a photo, then email it to me to prove you are genuine.

Romanticguy

What do you want me to write it with?

Danni

I dont care what you write it with, doesn't your wife have lipstick or something?

Romanticguy

Alright.

FROGS

When I was about ten, my best friend Dominic and I would go down to the creek at the end of our street and play. The creek contained thousands of tadpoles and you could easily find several frogs by lifting rocks.

Speaking of my best friend Dominic, he lived just five minutes from my house with grape vines between the houses. One day he called me to come over and I left right away. As I was walking through the grapevines, I received what felt like a large push from behind and almost fell, when I turned around to confront the person who had pushed me, there was nobody there. I continued to Dominic's house and he asked where I had been because I had left my house almost four hours earlier. True story. I have, to this day, no knowledge of where the four hours went but I think I walked through some kind of temporal distortion field, possibly to a far off future where I met my soul mate, grew old together and was then given the choice after she died to return to my own time, the moment I left, with no memory of my future life. This is obviously the most likely explanation.

We would take a frog and insert one of those thin fruit box straws into its anus and blow it up like a balloon. We would then put the frog onto the water and let go and watch it speed across the creek. Sometimes the frogs would burst as we were blowing them up. As the creeks were teeming with the tadpoles, we classed this as no more cruel and unnecessary as throwing the tadpoles at each other from each side of the creek in what we called tadpole wars. One day we threw frogs at cars driving past but were chased by a lady so we didn't do that again. Once, after reading that licking toads would make you high, we dared each other to swallow frogs live. On one occasion my mother opened the freezer to find eighteen frozen frogs because I had been told that they could be frozen and then revived.

A couple of years ago I was in the area with my son and we went to the creek but there were no frogs or tadpoles in it. This could be because they have all died out from pollution over the years but I prefer to think that they are fine and remembered me through some form of inherited group memory and hid. We did find a shopping trolley though which entertained my son for about an hour so that was good.

I thought I would have a lot more to write about frogs but I am bored already.

Frog Facts

The Brazilian Jungle Frog can mimic human speech and grows to the size of a small child.

Frozen frogs make a healthy and fun addition to any kid's school lunch box.

Mud Frogs can live for up to eighty years but spend all this time in hibernation under dried river mud.

When blended, frogs make an excellent energy drink which contains 92% of reccomended daily vitamin intake.

Frogs have excellent reception and can be used in place of your standard television aerial.

Placed between tissue paper and under heavy books for a few weeks, a dried frog makes a stunning broach.

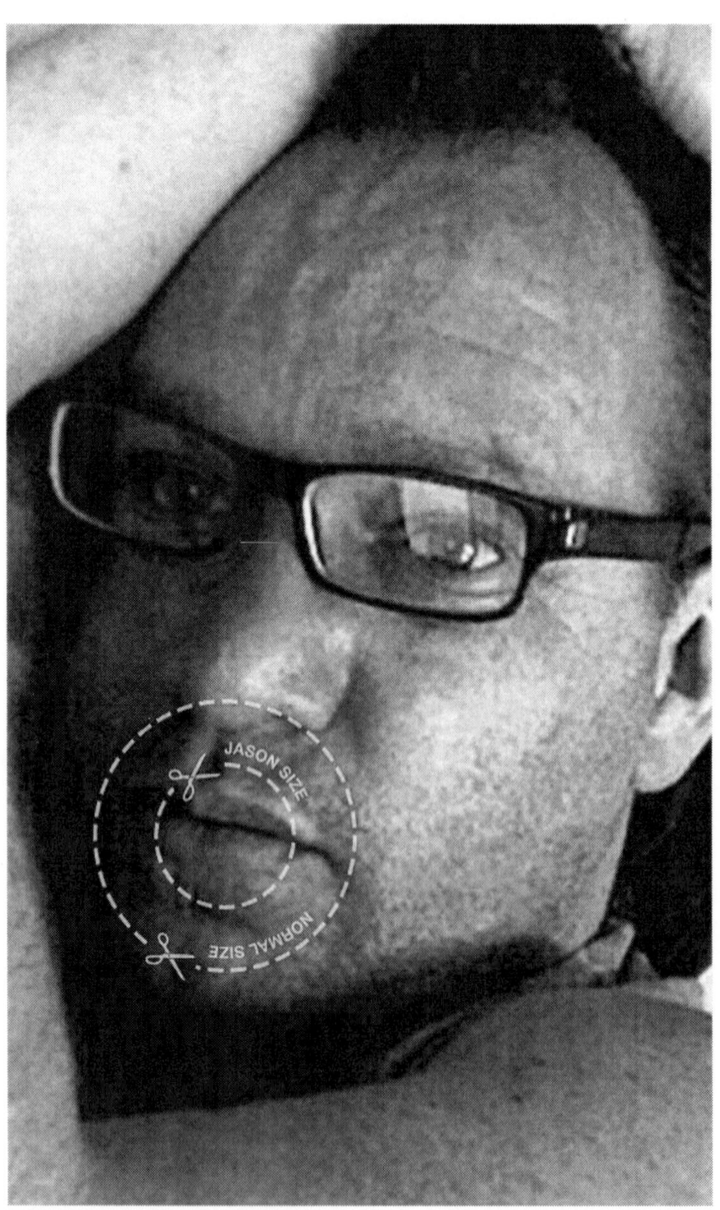

Handy fine art scanning template

SCANNING FINE ART WITH JASON
A STEP-BY-STEP GUIDE

Hello, my name is Jason and I scan fine art. People often ask me about the best techniques for scanning fine art and I have compiled this handy reference for successful fine art scanning.

I discovered fine art scanning when I was about twelve or thirteen. Around 97% of people, male and female, scan fine art regularly and it is a healthy and normal exercise. Those that do not are usually suffering mental or physical problems so it seems strange that fine art scanning is still seen as taboo or embarrassing these days and the term 'fine art scanner' derogatory. In actual fact the term 'non-fine art scanner' should be more insultive as it hints at a mental illness. Those that are required to scan fine art should be encouraged and commended on such a socially responsible activity.

Dear Jason

Q. *Dear Jason, sometimes I scan fine art when I am at work, is this normal or should I see someone about it? Thanks, Chris.*

A. Scanning fine art at work is completely normal Chris, I am currently scanning fine art as I write this. My favourite place to scan fine art is in public places such as movie theatres and playgrounds. Sometimes when I scan fine art I like to imagine I am on stage or speaking at a conference.

Q. *Dear Jason, Sometimes I think about firemen when I am scanning fine art. Is this normal? Rob.*

A. It is perfectly normal Rob, I often imagine I am a fire man or army man when I am scanning fine art.

Q. *Dear Jason, I have heard that scanning fine art too much can cause blindness. Is this true or did someone make that up? Cheers, Mike.*

A. Hello Mike, I can honestly say there is no truth to this rumour. I regularly scan fine art thirty to forty times a day with no negative results. Once, during back to back episodes of the Gilmore Girls, I scanned fine art one hundred and twelve times with no adverse effects.

Q. *Dear Jason, I am left handed and I was wondering if this will affect my ability to scan fine art effectively. Best, Steve.*

A. Being left handed is an advantage Steve, I myself am right handed but use my left leaving my mouse hand free.

Step 1 Take one roll of Oreo biscuits out of the packet and cut off end.

Step 2 Roll the end of the packet over several times until you have a smooth, rounded bevel.

Step 3 Choose a photo of someone you would like to scan fine art with. Place the packet bevel over the lips and trace around the circumference.

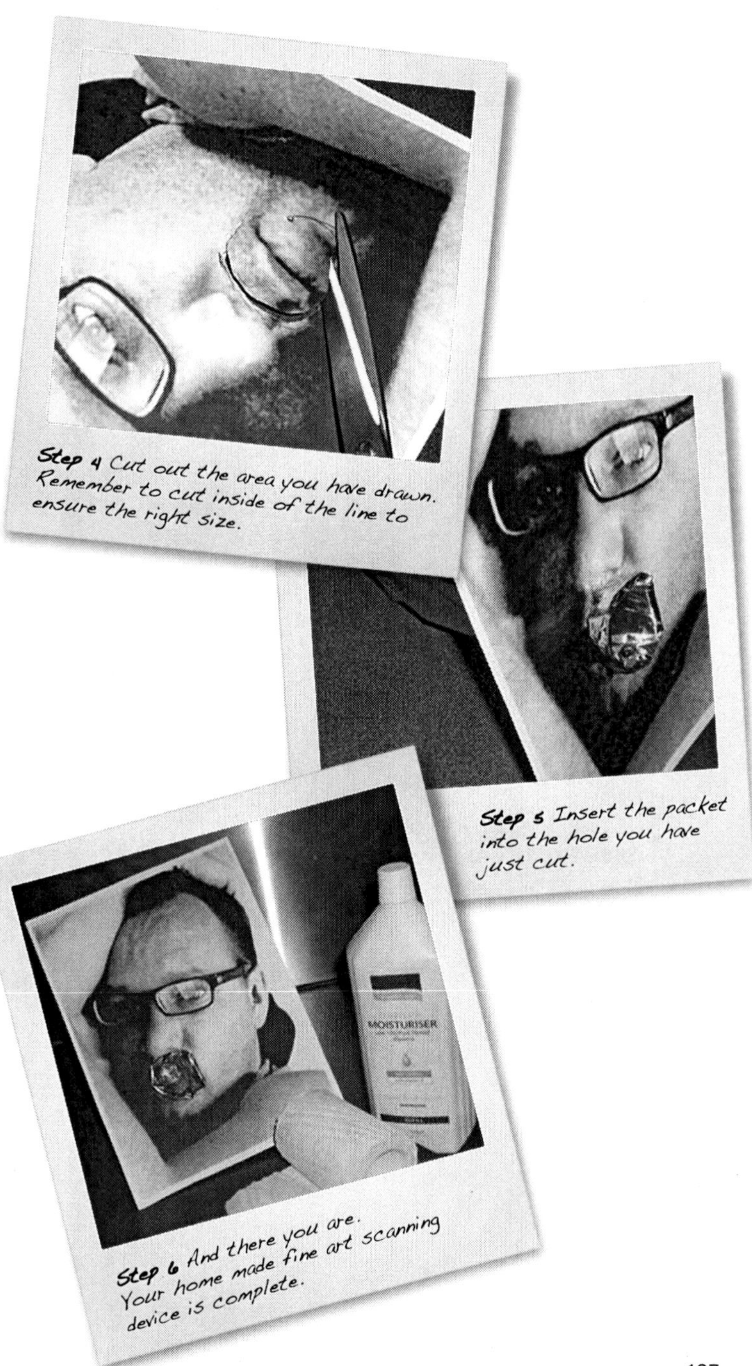

Step 4 Cut out the area you have drawn. Remember to cut inside of the line to ensure the right size.

Step 5 Insert the packet into the hole you have just cut.

Step 6 And there you are. Your home made fine art scanning device is complete.

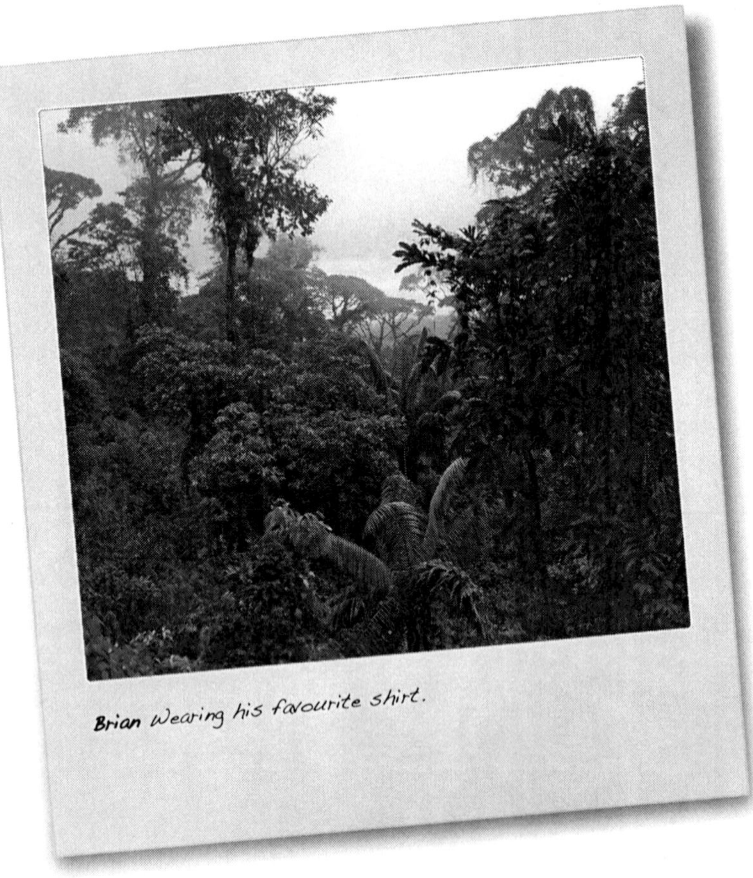
Brian wearing his favourite shirt.

OUTBACK BRIAN'S GUIDE TO WILDERNESS SURVIVAL

Hello, my name is Brian and I have been lost thirty six times which makes me an expert. Once when I was lost in the desert, I survived by absorbing the moisture from the air through my skin like a frog and feeding on krill. Another time when I was lost in the Antarctic, I fashioned a snowmobile from ice and rode to safety. I have compiled this complete guide to wilderness survival to ensure you too can survive, should you find yourself lost, in almost any environment.

Survival Tip #1

If you have water with you, drink it all immediately. There is a good chance you will be rescued before long so it is pointless being dehydrated. If you do run out of water, the trick to finding more in the wilderness is to remember that water always flows downhill. Find a hill and wait at the bottom. I read somewhere that if there is no water available, you can drink your own urine so I always take a two litre bottle of it wherever I go just in case.

Survival Tip #2

Do not eat the bright purple mushrooms. Once while lost, I found and ate some bright purple mushrooms figuring such a friendly colour could not possibly be dangerous. A short time later, a beetle and I discussed the differences between the director's cut of Bladerunner and the cinematic release. Always remember that bark is an excellent source of nutrition and can be prepared simply by marinating overnight and cooking for twenty minutes in a preheated oven at 240 degrees celcius.

Things that should not be eaten:

Bright purple mushrooms
Rocks
Cha-Chi's Mexican Restaurant food
Wasps

Survival Tip #3

Building yourself a shelter is an integral part of survival. A small bungalow or cottage will be sufficient unless you have a lot of furniture. Always remember that when tiling a roof, it is important to use a rope and harness to avoid falling. If you do fall, land horizontally with your arms and legs stretched out to maximise surface area. Always check with your local council on required permits prior to building. Protect yourself from hungry animals by fortifying your shelter. A wall of no less than two metres with a lockable gate should be sufficient. Always build your wall out of non combustible materials as wild animals will often attempt to gain access by using fire. Befriend large animals such as bears to protect you from smaller ones. A bear can easily be mollified by running towards it yelling.

Materials that are not suitable for building shelter with:

Water
Angry words
Live ants

Survival Tip #4

Building a fire without the use of matches or a lighter is a simple matter. Most forest fires are caused by lightning strikes so run a steel cable from the top of a tall tree to a pile of sticks and then be patient. Construct your fire under a group of trees and stack large piles of leaves around the edge to serve as wind breaks. Wolves are attracted to firelight but have a highly developed sense of smell and detest the odour of petrol so be sure to douse the surrounding area and yourself well.

If you do not have petrol with you and wolves enter your campsite, curling up into a small ball and making a high pitched sound like a wounded bird will confuse and deter them. If you are being attacked by a wolf, do not accidently grab a snake to fight it off with. If you have emergency flares, taping several dozen to your legs and setting them off at the same time will allow you to hover above the wolves for several seconds, safe from their snapping jaws.

Survival Tip #5

Having the appropriate clothing and medical equipment in preparation for any weather condition or emergency situation is the key to survival. If you are camping in a cool climate such as the Antarctic, make sure you take a scarf. Watching the movie Castaway will give you an idea of what items would be useful should you find yourself lost for several years and comes down to personal preference. If I was Tom Hanks, I would have taken several hundred cartons of cigarettes and a suitcase of pornography.

I read somewhere about a guy who, while camping, cut his leg and as he was sleeping, a spider laid eggs in the wound. I would rather amputate my leg than have baby spiders hatching in it so a surgical grade bone saw is an essential component in any backpack. It is always better to preempt these things so any limbs that receive cuts, scratches or bites should be removed immediately.

Survival Tip #6

Find some means of alerting rescuers to your whereabouts. If you are lost in a desert, writing a large SOS in the sand with your water is an effective means of drawing attention. If you are lost in a jungle, a simple two way radio can be constructed from kits available at any Tandy or RadioShack store. Waving your arms at passing rescue planes expends precious energy so it is better to dig a small hole, lay in it, cover yourself with leaves to keep warm and relax while you wait for them to find you.

Use the time you are waiting to be rescued wisely. Sort your DVD collection into alphabetical order or fix that broken tap that you have been meaning to for months but did get around to because it would mean driving to the hardware store and buying a new rubber washer. Scrapbooking is apparently a fun and satisfying hobby.

Having someone to talk to will help the time pass much more quickly. The last time I was lost and feeling lonely, I constructed company to talk to from mud. I called her Anne and after realising we had a lot in common, we fell in love. Sadly, she disappeared a few nights later during a rainstorm and though I searched desperately for her throughout the wilderness for many weeks, I eventually gave up hope and sought recluse from the outside world inside a dam where I lived for eight years with my pain and a family of angry beavers.

Survival Tip #7

If you become bored while waiting to be rescued and decide to walk, it is helpful to have a map. As you have no way of knowing where you may become lost, a map of everywhere is required. Simply marking everywhere on the map you are not will pinpoint where you are. A simple compass can be constructed by rubbing a small round pebble up and down polyester slacks to generate static magneticity then floating the pebble in a small pool of water. The pebble will sometimes face north.

Keeping a collection of pebbles in your pocket is also handy for when you come to a stream as you can use them as stepping stones. In case of deeper rivers, it is wise to carry a collection of larger rocks in your backpack at all times. If the river is still too deep, constructing a canoe can easily be accomplished by pouring a mixture of liquid polymer and setting agents into a precast mould.

CLOSED CIRCUIT TELEVISION CAMERA

The closed circuit television camera concealed in the front foyer records the hectic pace of a normal day in a busy design studio.

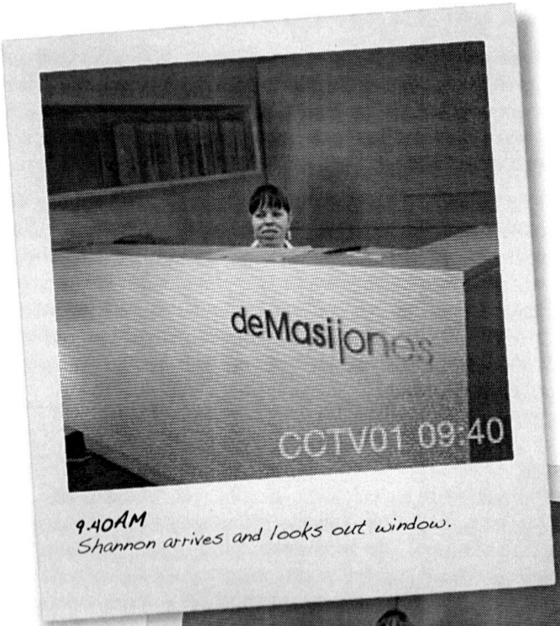

deMasijones

CCTV01 09:40

9.40AM
Shannon arrives and looks out window.

deMasijones

CCTV01 11:09

11.09AM
Shannon looks out window.

deMasi|jones
CCTV01 11:58
11.58AM
Shannon gets petty cash.
deMasi|jones
CCTV01 12:01
12.01PM
Shannon "pops out to get lunch
and do some things."

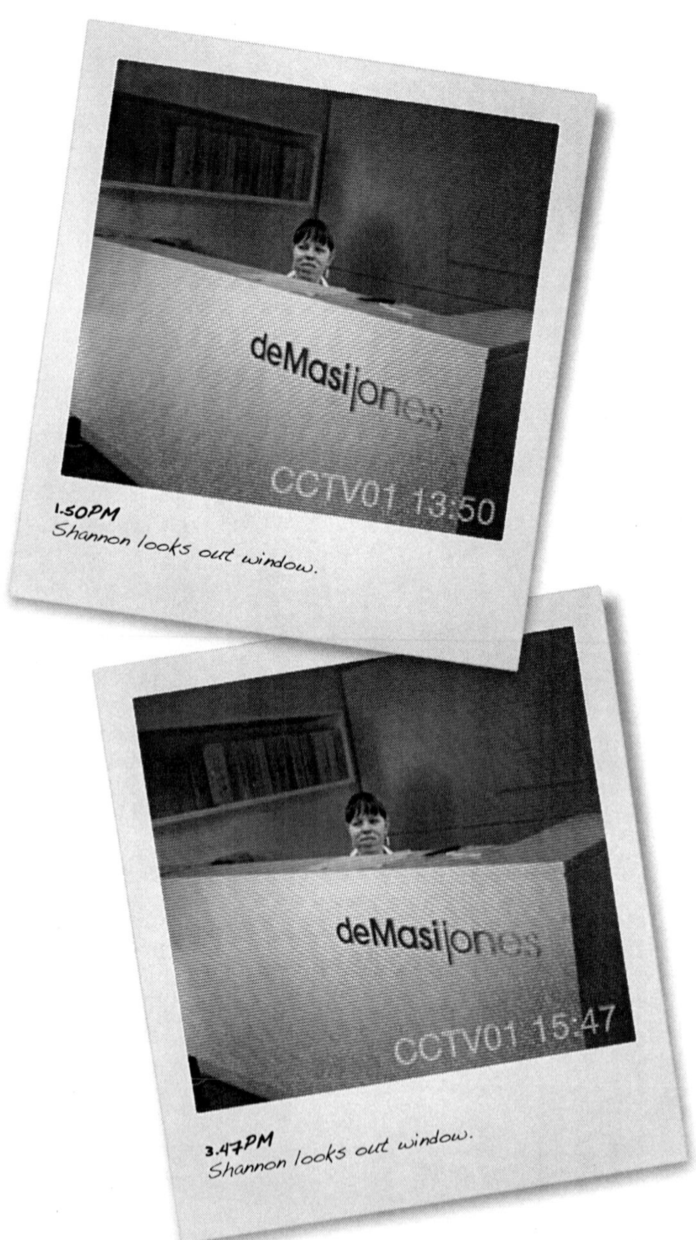
deMasi|jones
CCTV01 13:50
1.50PM
Shannon looks out window.
deMasi|jones
CCTV01 15:47
3.47PM
Shannon looks out window.

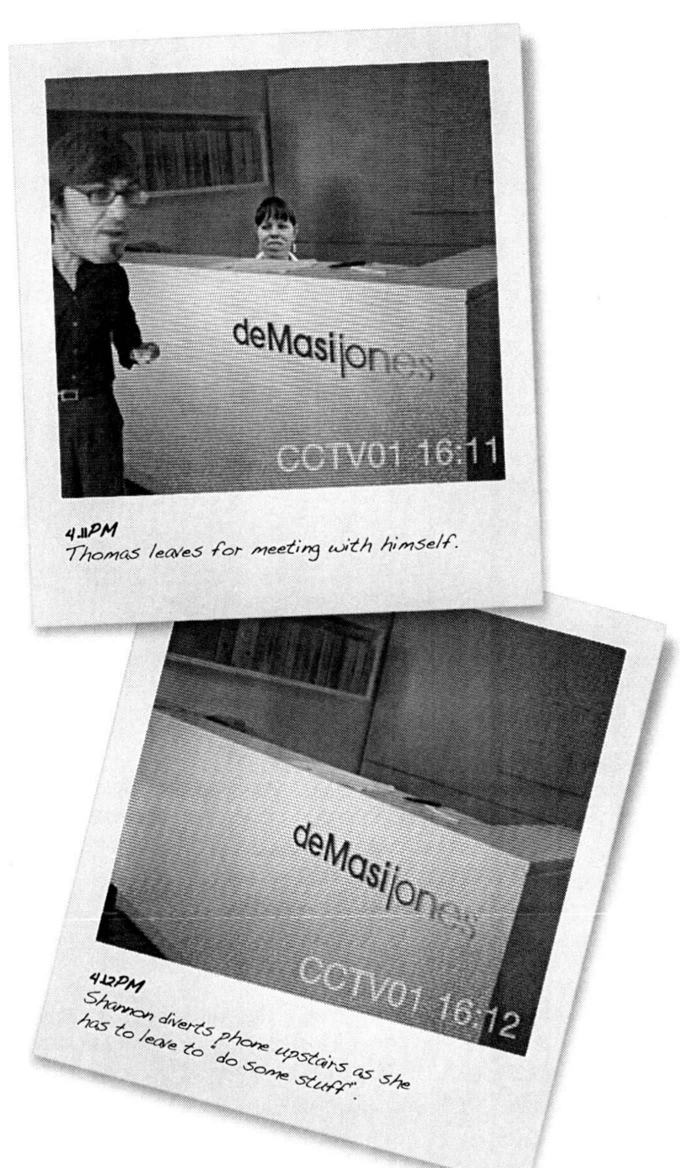
deMasi jones
CCTV01 16:11
4.11PM
Thomas leaves for meeting with himself.
deMasi jones
CCTV01 16:12
4.12PM
Shannon diverts phone upstairs as she has to leave to "do some stuff".

THE SA GREAT
DID YOU KNOW QUIZ

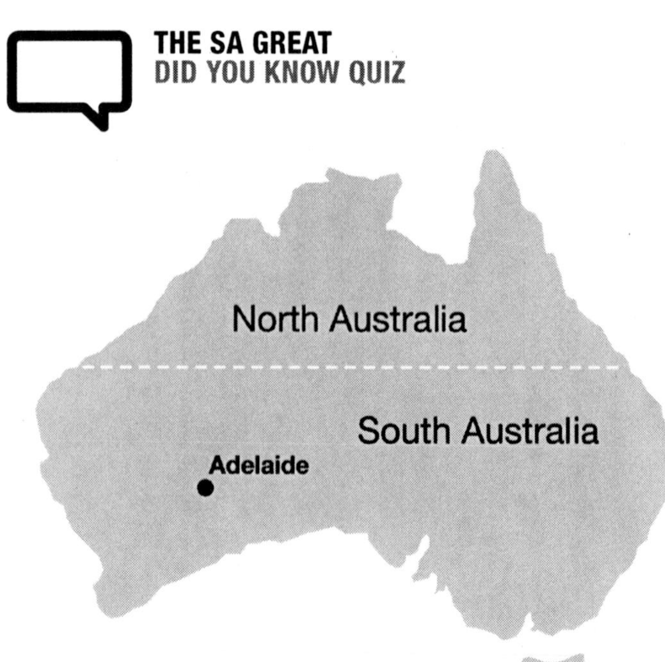

Question 1
Australian Idol winner Guy Sebastian studied at the Elder School of Music in Adelaide. For 5 points, what is the circumference of his head?

A. Huge
B. Ridiculous
C. Any bigger and it would require support pillars

Question 2
In 1998, South Australian astronaut Dr Andy Thomas took part in a mission on the NASA space shuttle Endeavor that required he spend 141 days in space. For 5 points, what was the relationship between Dr Smith and Will Robinson in lost in space?

A. Suspicious
B. Worrying
C. Special

Question 3

Jimmy Barnes from Cold Chisel was born in Elizabeth, South Australia. For 5 points, name the controversial abortion pill highlighted in media recently.

Question 4

The Adelaide Football Club, The Crows, has the highest membership in AFL. For 5 points, the George Orwell novel 1984 can best be described as:

A. A nightmarish dystopia where an omnipresent state enforces conformity
B. Party totalitarianism through indoctrination and fear.
C. One of the most influential pieces of literature of the twentieth century

Question 5

The Royal Adelaide Show receives the largest number of competitive entries in a show in the world. For 5 points which is the scariest part of the Royal Adelaide Show?

A. The ride that goes up and then round a bit.
B. That one that goes right over then stops.
C. The people operating the rides.

Question 6

Makybe Diva was the name of the mare from Port Lincoln that made history by winning back-to-back Melbourne Cups. For 5 points, the largest selling pet food product in Australia is:

A. Snappy Tom
B. Lucky Dog
C. Pal

Question 7

Golden Grove was awarded the International Real Estate Federation Award in 1998 that named it the "World's Best New Residential Development." For 5 points, what is the most popular garden decoration?

A. Concrete
B. Car bodies
C. Pot plants taken from other suburbs

Question 8
Humphey B. Bear, a much-loved Australian children's TV character starred in more than 3,000 episodes filmed in South Australia.
For 5 points, the show was canceled because:

A. Humphrey wasn't wearing pants
B. It was boring
C. Didn't involve a Japanese character who collects monsters

Question 9
Coopers Brewery is Australia's sole remaining family-owned brewery, now in its fourth generation? For 5 points, how many pints would you have to drink to find Thomas attractive.

A. 25
B. 50
C. Hook me up to a drip.

Question 10
Monarto Zoological Park is the only one in Australia to have successfully bred cheetahs in captivity. For 5 points, when driving through Monarto Zoo do you:

A. See an exciting range of exotic animals
B. Wonder where the animals are
C. Wonder what's on TV

Question 11
Balfours produce 15,000 meat pies per hour from their Dudley Park factory in South Australia. For 5 points, approximately how many different animals are in each pie?

A. 10+
B. 20+
C. The missing animals from Monarto Zoo

Question 12
South Australian designer, Gerry Wedd's designs have been associated with internationally recognised Australian clothing label Mambo.
For 5 points, how many designers does it take to change a lightglobe?

A. 1
B. 1 designer but four days of production meetings
C. 'I'm not changing anything.'

Question 13
Adelaide Festival Centre workshops created the system for Nikki Webster to 'fly' during the opening ceremony of the 2000 Sydney Olympics.
For 5 points, Nicki Webster should also have taken part in:

A. Skeet shooting
B. Javelin
C. Archery
D. All of the above as a target

Lesley Unicef sponsored woman golfer

LESLEY, THE ADVENTUROUS OUTDOORS TYPE
WITH A LOVE OF WATERSPORTS AND EVERYTHING OUTDOORS

Having received a love letter from Lesley in regards to the webpage about the poor black boy, I had a quick glance through his personal website. The website, written by Lesley, about Lesley and featuring several photos of Lesley, describes Lesley as "...the adventurous outdoors type with a love of watersports and everything outdoors". Wasps are outdoors Lesley, do you love wasps? Fuse boxes? Open cut mining? Pedestrian crossings?

Things that people have emailed me that are outdoors and therefore Lesley loves:

Traffic lights, Prickles, Litter, A bus, My sister Amanda, Flies, Cigarette butts, Land mines, Homeless people, Sticks,Grandma, Dark alleyways, Bins, Opera in the park, Feral cats, Playgrounds, Dust, Used condoms, Fat people at hot dog stands, Blowfish, Construction workers, Snipers, Shade, Airborne viruses, Mandy says Toilets, A box, Shoes because of the carpet, A Wading Pool, Children on a field trip, Astro-turf®, Lesley, Indians on public transport, Holes in fences, Tether Ball, Starving 3rd world children, My poodle Benny, Quicksand, Lawn Sausages, For Sale signs, Boy Scouts, Peeping Toms, Lawn furniture, Flagpoles, Television Antenna's, Owl pellets, Street walkers, Forest fires, Techno Viking, Public Toilets, Yellow Snow, Speed bumps, Lost kittens, Free Candy Vans, Cement, Garden Gnomes...

From: Les Copeland
Date: Thursday 15 Jan 2009 4.19pm
To: David Thorne
Subject: Poor black boy

What kind of a complete fucking moron makes fun of starving children? What a pathetic attempt at humour. I have spent time in third world countries and seen children starving with my own eyes and I think you seriously need to grow the fuck up.

Les

From: David Thorne
Date: Thursday 15 Jan 2009 6.41pm
To: Les Copeland
Subject: Re: Poor black boy

Dear Lesley,

Thankyou for your kind email, I am glad you enjoyed the website. In answer to your question, no I cannot send you a photo of myself without a shirt on. I have however attached this photo of a mouse riding on a toads back. It is a visual metaphor for how you must have felt writing that last email; magnanimous, the world on your shoulders and moist.

Regards, David.

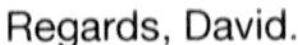

From: Les Copeland
Date: Friday 16 Jan 2009 10.28am
To: David Thorne
Subject: Re: Re: Poor black boy

Are you fucking retarted? Where did I ask for a photo of you? I wrote to you about the poor black boy page. As If I would want a photo of someone who thinks starving children are funny. You need a punch in the head. And my name isnt Lesley moron. Tell me where you live and we will see how fucking funny
you are.

Les

From: David Thorne
Date: Friday 16 Jan 2009 11.02am
To: Les Copeland
Subject: Re: Re: Re: Poor black boy

Dear Lesbian,

Thankyou for your request but I regret that I am unable to provide you with an address as I am homeless. Please send money and/or Lego. I have been collecting lego blocks for nearly four years now as I intend to build my own home. I currently have exactly 1,692,008 blocks of various sizes and only need another 4,836,029 to complete plans of constructing a four bedroom home with sunken lounge and indoor swimming pool. Prior plans to build a home from seawater were abandoned due to physics. The advantages of using lego blocks over traditional building methods, in regards to durability and gaiety of colour, are without question. The only issues are finding a block of land that has a flat green plastic base and gaining council approval but that should not prove a major obstacle as my local member of parliament, Kate Ellis, Planet Earth's sexiest space politician, is not adverse to a bribe. Kate Beckinsale is the only other attractive lesbian politician I can think of. The rest are just appalling. I have attached a photo of Kate Ellis as a sexy space girl in case you do not know who she is.

Regards, David.

From: Les Copeland
Date: Saturday 17 Jan 2009 2.09pm
To: David Thorne
Subject: Re: Re: Re: Re: Poor black boy

I have no idea who the fuck that is and it wouldnt suprise me if you were homeless loser. spending your time writing shit like that instead of getting a real job like a grown up what are you 15? Did your mummy buy you the computer you are using? Why dont you turn off your computer and go outdoors there is a whole world out there. and Les is short for Lester moron.
I seriously want to punch you in the fucking face.

From: David Thorne
Date: Saturday 17 Jan 2009 2.37pm
To: Les Copeland
Subject: Re: Re: Re: Re: Re: Poor black boy

Dear moLester,

I appreciate the suggestion but dislike the outdoors, it has bees and sharp sticks in it. Once, when I went camping with my sister and brother, my sister became angry at a comment I made regarding her girth and drove off leaving us stranded two hundred and thirty kilometres from the nearest McDonalds. By the third day we tried eating grass and fought over a small lizard on the fourth. If you and I had known each other then, you could have arranged an emergency Unicef food parcel drop. As it was, we survived only by making love to keep warm and building a vehicle out of our clothing which enabled us to reach the nearest town where we danced for food.

You and I should go camping together some time as you seem like an adventurous, outdoors kind of guy with a love of watersports and everything outdoors. I read somewhere about a father and son who went camping and during the night a tree branch fell on their tent killing the child so I always sleep the furthest distance possible from my son when we are camping together. Safety first. You would be a handy person to have along in case we became lost as we could use your Village People moustache as kindling to create a signal fire and your naturally reflective surface to alert search planes.

In regards to getting a real job, my current position as assistant to the managing assistant in charge of envelopes fills much of my spare time and I have been promised a promotion to assistant to the assistant manager in charge of assistants within ten years. The corporate stepladder has my name on every rung. Also, I understand your need to assert yourself physically, I too can only experience true intimacy through pain. As I have ventured onto your website and seen your photo, my only requirement would be that we keep the lights off as imagination has its limits. I have had worse of course, my last girlfriend was the poster girl for 'love is blind' and my current partner is overseas at the moment so the only intimacy in my life involves a stick of salami and the neigbors dog when Glenda & Frank go out Tuesday nights.

Once when they arrived home early due to an argument between them regarding Frank's internet usage, I hid in their wardrobe for four days. As I could see Frank using his computer from my hiding position, I can vouch for his denials to Glenda's accusations that he was "looking at girls on the intenet". He was looking at photos of her. No not really, it was men.

To prime myself for your proximity, I have printed your photo out and have it sitting on the couch next to me while we watch a DVD together. Occassionally, I throw an M&M at you and pretend you giggle and tell me to stop it. We are watching Nanny Mcphee which always makes me cry. The bit at the end where her wedding dress materialises out of snow is simply beautiful but my favourite scene is where the robots turn on their human masters.

Regards, David.

From: Les Copeland
Date: Saturday 17 Jan 2009 6.41pm
To: David Thorne
Subject: Re: Re: Re: Re: Re: Re: Poor black boy

You are a complete idiot. Dont email me again.

From: David Thorne
Date: Saturday 17 Jan 2009 6.57pm
To: Les Copeland
Subject: Re: Re: Re: Re: Re: Re: Re: Poor black boy

ok

From: Les Copeland
Date: Saturday 17 Jan 2009 7.02pm
To: David Thorne
Subject: Re: Re: Re: Re: Re: Re: Re: Re: Poor black boy

Fuck off

ABOUT THE AUTHOR

David Thorne works in the design and branding industry as design director for a small Adelaide design agency as he is too lazy and easily distracted to do a real job. Amongst the multitude of his qualities, which include reciting prime numbers backwards from 909526, reading to blind children and training guide dogs, embellishment may be at the top.

David lives with his partner (who recently made the top 100 on *So You Think You Can Dance*) in Adelaide, South Australia, which is commonly regarded as the murder capital of Australia. This title is given to Adelaide not due to the volume of murders, but due to the clever antics of Adelaide's finest serial killers. Ironically, Adelaide is the only Australian capital city not founded by convicts.

David reads too much, generally exceeds others' tolerances and listens to *Linkin Park*. He stays up too late, drinks too much coffee, smokes too much, hates getting up in the morning and has offspring who thinks David doesn't know what he has been up to when he deletes his internet history.

Lightning Source UK Ltd.
Milton Keynes UK
UKOW041816291012

201380UK00001B/60/P